Melody and Rhythm

Melody and Rhythm
Semester 3

Bill Stevens
Director of Musicianship
Santa Clara University
billstevens.net

An Avivo Publication
www.avivo.com

Copyright © 2018 by Bill Stevens. All Rights Reserved.
Edited by Dr. Loretta Notareschi
Copy editing by Reilly Farrell
Cover design by Steve Kusmer

Contents

Acknowledgements vii

About the Author ix

Introduction 1

13 Irregular Rhythms   3
13.1 Three in the Time of Two, Two in the Time of Three 4
13.2 Four in the Time of Three, Three in the Time of Four 13
13.3 Three Against Four 22

14 Basic Key Relationships   33
14.1 Parallel and Relative Major/Minor 34
14.2 Tonicizing the Dominant 49
14.3 Modulating to the Dominant 60
14.4 More Movement to the Dominant 73

15 Changing Meters   87
15.1 Changing Like Meters 88
15.2 Mixing Simple and Compound with a
     Constant Division 95
15.3 Mixing Simple and Compound with a
     Constant Beat 102

16 More Key Relationships   111
16.1 Tonicizing the Subdominant 112
16.2 Modulating to the Subdominant 126
16.3 Secondary Key Relationships in Major 140
16.4 Secondary Key Relationships in Minor 153

17 Odd and Composite Meters   169
17.1 Quintuple and Septuple Meters 170
17.2 Composite Meters 178
17.3 Changing Composite Meters 186

18 Modes of the Major Scale — 195
18.1 Lydian and Dorian — 198
18.2 Mixolydian and Phrygian — 208
18.3 Modal Melodies Written in the Parallel Major Key — 219
18.4 Modal Melodies Written in the Parallel Minor Key — 230

Acknowledgements

Developing the *Melody and Rhythm* curriculum has been a labor of love spanning several years. I have had help from a team of extraordinary people. Foremost, I want to thank my editor, Dr. Loretta Notareschi, whose discerning eye and meticulous attention to detail have been extremely valuable.

I am vastly grateful to my copy editor and notation assistant, Reilly Farrell, whose staunch reliability and deep willingness to tackle any problem have been absolutely invaluable.

I want to warmly thank my proofreader team: Margaret Simons, Lydia Davidson, Nicole Yazmin Jacobus, and Anne Hsia. (Any errors that remain are my own.)

I would also like to warmly thank my Avivo colleague and mentor Dr. Pam Quist for a lifetime of friendship, for helping me to shape the overall structure of this course, and for many delightful lunches over Thai food.

I have had the great fortune to learn musicianship and sight singing from fantastic models. In particular, I want to thank Patricia Plude and Leo Wanenchak, whose deep love of learning and willingness to pass along the fruits of their learning to other teachers are priceless.

I also want to thank Phi Lam and Kevin Yee for many hours spent poring through recordings and scores with me; Phi Lam for assistance finding folk melodies; Chris Nalls for lots of encouragement, feedback, and photo-copying; Leland Kusmer for developing the LaTeX package for this book; Steve Kusmer for designing the cover and title page; Dr. Shawn Crouch for help pacing the harmonic content; Chip Newton for feedback about lead sheet formatting; Dr. Scot Hanna-Weir for suggesting that I include examples with figured bass and harmonic analysis; Michael Howell for assistance navigating the world of contemporary popular music; Hans Boepple and John Kennedy for loaning books and recordings; and members of the Lilypond-Users group for assistance troubleshooting various notation issues.

I want to thank Phyllis Magal and Dr. Lynn Hillberg Jencks for lots of good energy and for helping me talk through many of the decisions that went into this text.

I want to thank the College of Arts and Sciences at Santa Clara University for supporting research for this book with several Dean's Grants.

Lastly, thank you to Carla and Tom Stevens for a lifetime of encouragement and support.

About the Author

Bill Stevens directs the musicianship program at Santa Clara University. He is a founding member of Avivo, a collective of master educators dedicated to cultivating creativity through music teaching, and served on the faculty of The Walden School for twelve years. Bill is the author of *Jazz Musicianship: A Guidebook for Integrated Learning*. He has performed as a guest pianist with The Silkroad Ensemble. Bill is a recipient of the prestigious Presidential Scholars Award and was a Level 1 Finalist with NFAA (now YoungArts) in music composition. Curious about the relationship between creativity, learning, and psychological process, Bill studied psychotherapy with the Helix Training Program and is a certified Somatic Experiencing Practitioner. Learn more at his website: www.billstevens.net.

Introduction

This is the third of four semesters of the *Melody and Rhythm* curriculum, comprising Chapters 13 through 18. Rhythmically, we will work with irregular rhythms (such as quadruplets and three against four) in Chapter 13, changing meters in Chapter 15, and odd and composite meters in Chapter 17. Melodically, we will begin by connecting material from two different key areas, working with basic key relationships in Chapter 14 and more key relationships in Chapter 16. In Chapter 18 we will tackle scales other than major and minor, introducing the modes of the major scale.

In my own teaching, I take five weeks of class time for each rhythm and melody chapter pair. I cover a section from each chapter during weeks one through four, reserving week five to assess student learning. As rhythm chapters only have three sections while melody chapters have four, I use the fourth week for extra practice with rhythm duets, which tend to have a steeper learning curve.

The materials in Semester 3 are intended to be compatible with all systems of pitch and rhythm pedagogy. I will continue to use a specific set of rhythm syllables. If you prefer a different system, simply use that instead. There are a few places in melody chapters where material might best be approached differently depending on which pitch system you are using. I will offer specific advice about this when such occasions arise.

I encourage you to continue to explore variations in your practice routines. Go deep with dynamics and articulations. What if no two notes in any particular example were to have exactly the same dynamic or inflection? Play with affect. How would a melody be sung by someone you know who has lots of personality? By your favorite comedian? By your favorite cartoon character? Seek to embody the spirit of each example in your performance. How much can you communicate with timbre and nuance while rendering the pitches and rhythms accurately?

As always, I hope that this course continues to serve your growth. I hope that it challenges you and stretches your skills. I hope that it showcases music that you love and introduces you to music that is as yet unfamiliar. Mostly, I hope that it deepens both your passion for music and your respect for the craft of being a musician.

Bill Stevens
May 2018
Santa Clara, California

Chapter 13

Irregular Rhythms

Thus far, we have been exploring rhythmic vocabulary that works within the basic structure of the meter. Each bar has beats. Some beats have more weight than others. Beats can be divided and subdivided in various ways. Maybe the bar has three beats, maybe it has two. Maybe the beat is divided in two parts, maybe in three. Either way, the meter governs the basic structure of the rhythm.

Sometimes, though, the content of a rhythm clashes with the structure of the meter. This can happen in many ways. Perhaps three beats are squeezed into the space allotted for two beats. Perhaps three beats are stretched to fit the space allotted for four beats. Perhaps the beat is divided into four subdivisions that are accented in groups of three. Or perhaps the beat is divided into three and four equal parts at the same time. All of these rhythms clash with the basic structure of the meter and are known as "irregular rhythms." In this chapter, we will work with those irregular rhythms that mix groupings of two, three, and four.

Big triplets fill two beats. Huge triplets fill four beats.

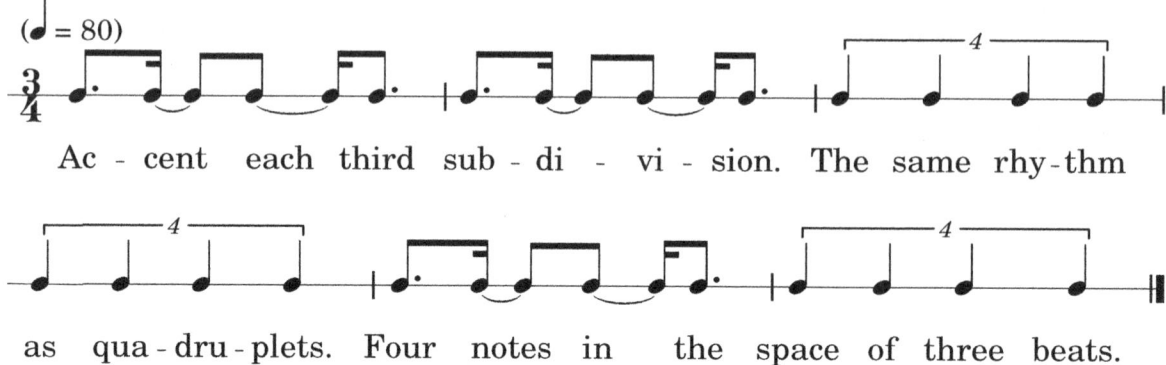

Ac - cent each third sub - di - vi - sion. The same rhy-thm as qua - dru - plets. Four notes in the space of three beats.

13.1 Three in the Time of Two, Two in the Time of Three

Our first irregular rhythm fits three equally-sized durations into the space of two beats. This is easiest to feel in compound meter, so we will begin there.

Three in the Time of Two in Compound Meter

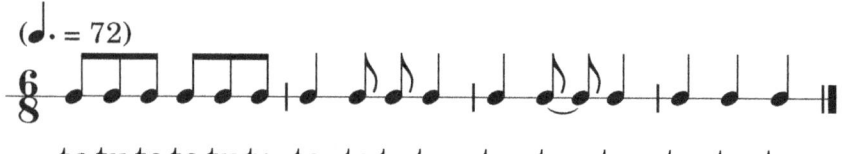

ta tu te ta tu te ta te ta tu ta te tu ta te tu

13.1. THREE IN THE TIME OF TWO, TWO IN THE TIME OF THREE

13.1a

In simple meter, three in the time of two requires a triplet bracket.

Three in the Time of Two in Simple Meter

13.1b

I've intentionally left all dynamic and articulation indications out of rhythm Examples C and D throughout this course. Practice interpreting these rhythms in different ways. Play with loud and soft. Play with up and down (non-specific changes in pitch). Play with articulation and with timbre. Play with sudden changes and with gradual changes. I've added the "Interpret" flag to these examples to invite you to play with interpretation here.

13.1c Interpret

13.1. THREE IN THE TIME OF TWO, TWO IN THE TIME OF THREE

13.1d Interpret

Lazy march ($\hbox{\textonehalf}=92$)

13.1e

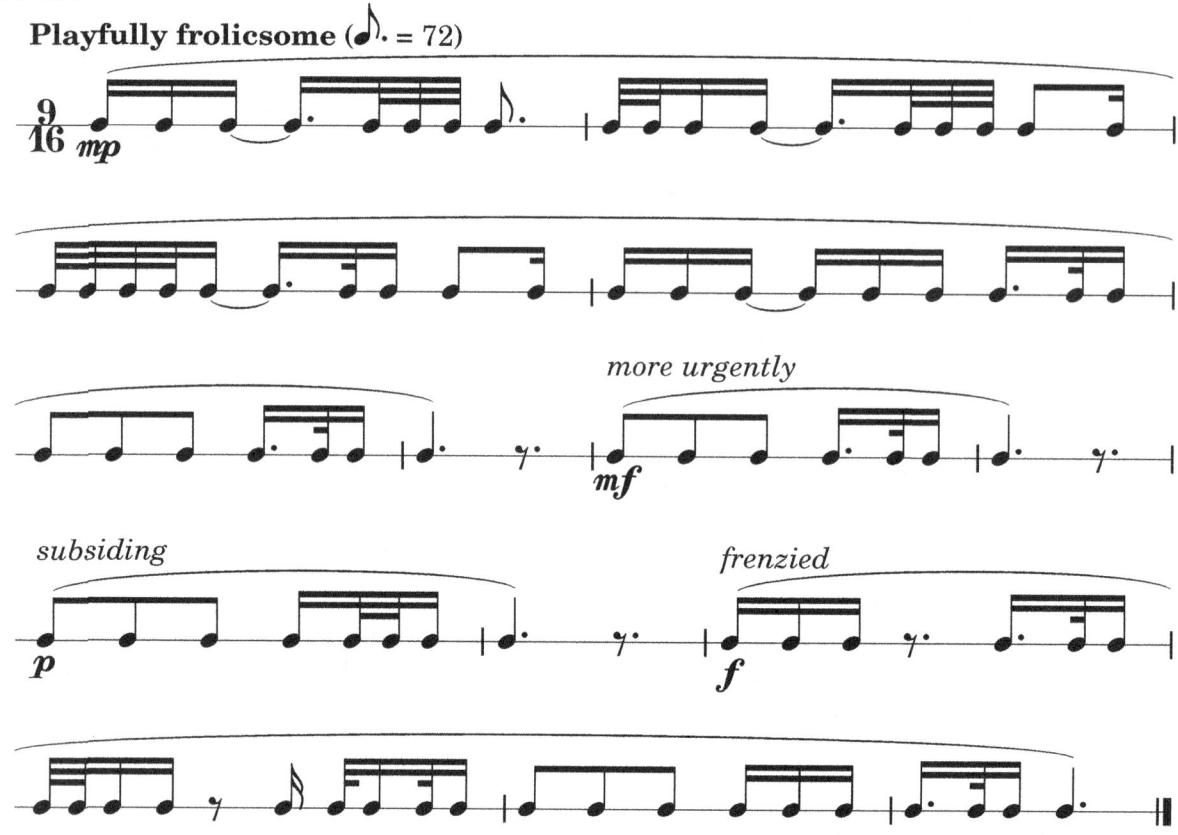

We can also fit two durations in the time of three beats. This is done easily enough using dotted rhythms and need not be a big deal, as in Example G. It gets interesting, however, when there are more or fewer than three beats in a bar, as in Example F.

13.1f

13.1. THREE IN THE TIME OF TWO, TWO IN THE TIME OF THREE

13.1g

13.1h

13.1. THREE IN THE TIME OF TWO, TWO IN THE TIME OF THREE

13.1i

Parlante ($\dot{\jmath}$. = 72)

13.1j

13.2 Four in the Time of Three, Three in the Time of Four

Our first three examples explore dividing four beats into three equal parts. In Example A, a full bar of 12/8 is filled with three half notes. In Example B, the half notes require a triplet bracket. Example C explores the same concept in 4/8 meter.

When dividing a four-beat bar into three long durations like this, give particular attention to the placement of the second and third durations. The second will come close to the beat just before it, and the third close to the beat to follow. This is easiest to hear at first in the context of compound meter, so we will start there.

Three in the Time of Four in Compound Meter

Three in the Time of Four in Simple Meter

13.2. FOUR IN THE TIME OF THREE, THREE IN THE TIME OF FOUR

Our next irregular rhythm involves fitting four durations into the time of three beats. When each beat is subdivided into groups of four, there are twelve total subdivisions in three beats. Dividing twelve subdivisions into four equal parts yields four durations of three subdivisions each. These can be written with dotted rhythms and ties, or by bracketing four equal durations under a number 4, indicating quadruplets.

Quadruplets in Simple Meter

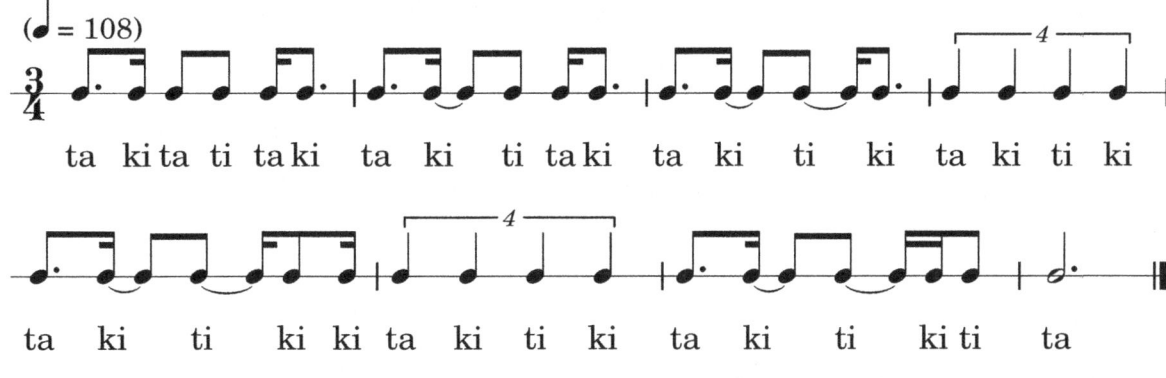

13.2d Interpret

Lackadaisically (♩ = 80)

13.2e

Quadruplets can also be found in compound meter, dividing a single beat into four durations rather than three. Common practice in such cases is to notate the quadruplets as subdivisions of the beat: four sixteenth notes filling a beat of 6/8 time for example, or four quadruplet eighth notes filling a beat of 6/4.

Quadruplets in Compound Meter

13.2. FOUR IN THE TIME OF THREE, THREE IN THE TIME OF FOUR

13.2f

Wistfully ($\dot{\mathstrut}$. = 56)

13.2g

Allegro con vivo (♪. = 120)

13.2. FOUR IN THE TIME OF THREE, THREE IN THE TIME OF FOUR

13.2h

Andantino (♩ = 92)

CHAPTER 13. IRREGULAR RHYTHMS

13.2i

Energico (♩ = 100)

13.2. FOUR IN THE TIME OF THREE, THREE IN THE TIME OF FOUR

13.2j

13.3 Three Against Four

Now, we'll work with groups of three and groups of four at the same time. Here, it is generally best not to focus too explicitly on the mechanics of how these two rhythms line up in time. Instead, cultivate the skill of feeling both rhythms independently at the same time.

Maintaining a steady pulse, practice going back and forth between dividing the beat into three parts and dividing the beat into four parts. Do this until both are deeply grounded and you can make the transition without a hitch. Then, try dividing the beat into three and four at the same time, speaking one part and tapping the other. This will likely feel awkward at first; give it time. You may find it helpful to use the feel of two against three as a stepping stone. Have this rhythm in your head as part of the background as you work to master three against four. As you become comfortable with this exercise, change speeds to keep your mind engaged.

13.3a

13.3. THREE AGAINST FOUR

13.3b
Lent (♩ = 54)

13.3c Interpret

13.3. THREE AGAINST FOUR

13.3d Interpret

CHAPTER 13. IRREGULAR RHYTHMS

13.3e

13.3. THREE AGAINST FOUR

13.3f

13.3g

13.3. THREE AGAINST FOUR

13.3h

13.3i

Intensely ($\d = 88$)

13.3. THREE AGAINST FOUR

13.3j

Chapter 14

Basic Key Relationships

We have worked with chromatic ornaments — hearing chromatic tones in relationship to the diatonic notes a half step away — and we have worked with chromatic skips — hearing chromatic notes independently. Now, we expand on our exploration of melodic chromaticism by connecting materials from two different key areas. Sometimes a composer does this by formally changing keys, introducing a new key signature in the middle of a piece of music. Sometimes a composer will simply use accidentals, implying the new key without actually changing the key signature. We will encounter examples of both in this chapter.

When a new key is introduced briefly, it is called tonicization. When a piece is mostly in one key with a momentary allusion to a different key, that's tonicization. When the key shifts for a more extended period of time, it is called modulation. If a piece is in one key and shifts to another key and stays in that new key for more than a few bars, that's modulation.

In this chapter, we will explore the most common ways of connecting material from two keys. In Section 1, we will work with parallel and relative major/minor key relationships. In Sections 2 through 4, we will practice moving to the key of the dominant: moving to five. Section 2 will focus on tonicizing five, Section 3 will explore modulating to five, and Section 4 will feature a mixture of tonicizing and modulating examples.

CHAPTER 14. BASIC KEY RELATIONSHIPS

14.1 Parallel and Relative Major/Minor

I recommend different approaches to this section depending on which pitch system you are using. If you are using numbers, fixed do, or note names, then treat this section like any other: spend some time with examples from each of the first three subsections, seasoning your practice with Specialty and Listening examples as desired.

If you have been using movable do with la-based minor, then I encourage you to use Examples A through H as a chance to practice do-based minor. Treat do as the tonic of the minor scale and use a lowered third, sixth, and seventh where appropriate: do-re-me-fa-sol-le-te-do. The do-based minor system naturally reinforces the parallel major/minor relationship of keys.

If you have been using movable do with do-based minor, then I encourage you to use Examples I through M as a chance to practice la-based minor. Treat do as the tonic of the major key and la as the tonic of the minor key a minor third below. This gives a natural minor scale of la-ti-do-re-mi-fa-sol-la. The la-based minor system reinforces the relative major/minor relationship of keys.

From Major to the Parallel Minor

One of the most basic ways to mix material from two different keys is to connect major and minor keys sharing the same tonic: C major and C minor, for example. This is called a "parallel" key relationship. We say that C minor is the "parallel minor" of C major and that C major is the "parallel major" of C minor. Here, examples are written in major, introducing the minor sound with accidentals for the lowered third, sixth, and seventh scale degrees.

14.1a

Symphony No. 2 in D major, Op. 36

Ludwig van Beethoven

14.1. PARALLEL AND RELATIVE MAJOR/MINOR

14.1b

Carnaval, Op. 9 - No. 14, Reconnaissance
Robert Schumann

14.1c

Vier Lieder für das Pianoforte, Op. 6 - No. 2
Fanny Mendelssohn

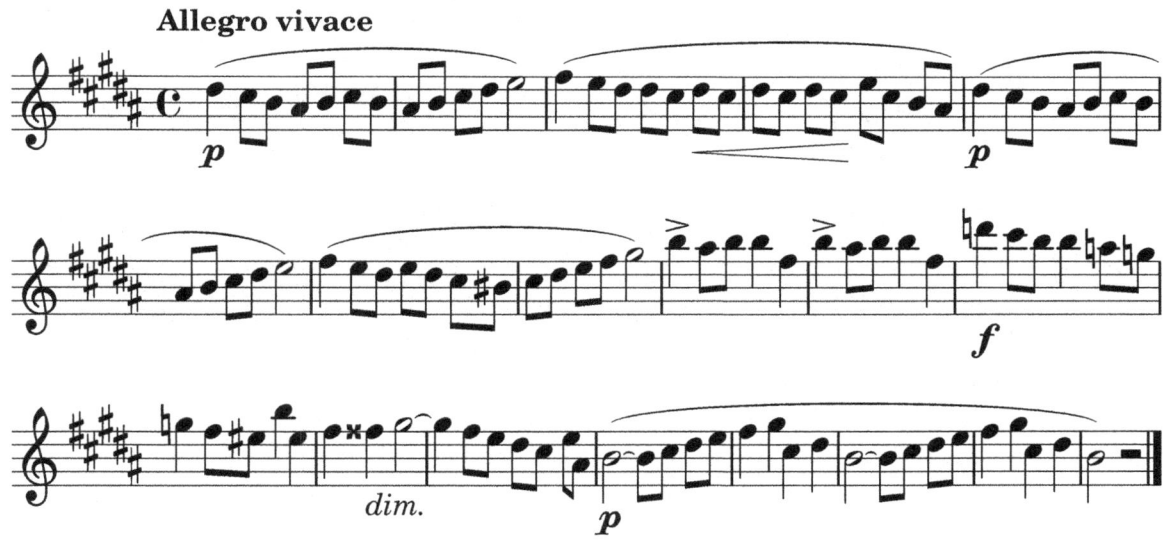

14.1d

The Gondoliers: Gavotte

Arthur Sullivan

14.1. PARALLEL AND RELATIVE MAJOR/MINOR

From Minor to the Parallel Major

Here, examples are written in minor. Examples E and F introduce the parallel major with accidentals raising the third, sixth, and seventh degrees. Examples G and H introduce the parallel major with a key change.

14.1e

Lied des gefangenen Jägers, D. 843

Franz Schubert

CHAPTER 14. BASIC KEY RELATIONSHIPS

14.1f

Schwanengesang, D. 957 - No. 4, Ständchen

Franz Schubert

14.1g

14.1. PARALLEL AND RELATIVE MAJOR/MINOR

14.1h

Hélène Polka

Alexander Borodin

Relative Major/Minor

In this subsection, we connect major and minor keys that share the same key signature. This is called a "relative" key relationship. We say that C major is the "relative major" of A minor because both C major and A minor have a key signature of no sharps or flats. We also say that A minor is the "relative minor" of C major.

14.1i

Come, Lasses and Lads

Traditional

14.1j

Quintet für 2 Violinen, Viola, Violoncell und Klavier

Alexander Borodin

14.1. PARALLEL AND RELATIVE MAJOR/MINOR

14.1k

Peer Gynt Suite No. 1, Op. 46 - No. 1, Morning Mood

Edvard Grieg

14.1l

Carmen - Toreador Song

Georges Bizet

14.1. PARALLEL AND RELATIVE MAJOR/MINOR

14.1m

Mazurka in B minor, WoO 15

Alexander Scriabin

Specialty Examples

Study the examples in this subsection carefully to determine which feature relative and which feature parallel major/minor relationships.

14.1n Duet

Serenade for Strings, Op. 22

Antonín Dvořák

14.1. PARALLEL AND RELATIVE MAJOR/MINOR

14.1o Jam Session

Rain and sunshine (♩ = 104)

14.1p Analysis

Invention in A minor, BWV 784

Johann Sebastian Bach

14.1q Figured Bass

14.1. PARALLEL AND RELATIVE MAJOR/MINOR

14.1r Lead Sheet

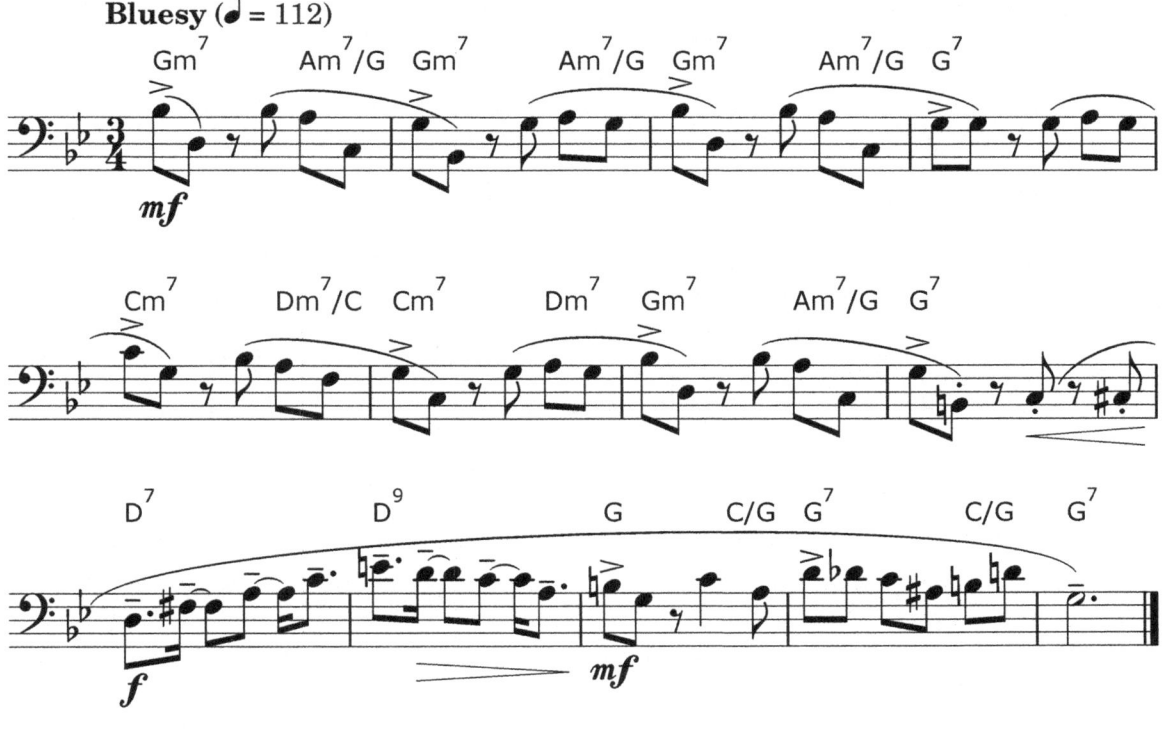

14.1s Find the Music

14.1t Fill in the Blanks

Listening Examples

Relative Major/Minor

- Jazz: Clifford Brown, "Jordu," from *Clifford Brown and Max Roach* (0:00–0:15), head by Duke Jordan.

- Television: Jack Marshall and Bob Mosher, theme from "The Munsters."

- Rock: The Beatles, "Girl," from *Rubber Soul* (0:00–0:37), written by John Lennon and Paul McCartney. Listen for the shift to the relative major in the harmonic accompaniment to the voice.

- Rock: Fleetwood Mac, "You Make Loving Fun," from *Rumours*, written by Christine McVie.

Parallel Major/Minor

- Jazz: Art Farmer, "Jubilation," from *Modern Art* (0:00–0:55), head by Junior Mance.

- Rock: The Beatles, "Mean Mr. Mustard," from *Abbey Road*, written by John Lennon and Paul McCartney.

- Rock: The Beatles, "Lady Madonna," from *Past Masters*, written by John Lennon and Paul McCartney.

- Pop: Barbra Streisand, "When in Rome I Do as the Romans Do," from *People*, written by Cy Coleman and Carolyn Leigh.

- Folk: Joni Mitchell, "A Little Green," from *Blue*.

- Alternative: They Might Be Giants, "Birdhouse in Your Soul," from *Flood* (0:15–0:31), written by John Flansburgh and John Linnell.

- Television: Ramin Djawadi, theme from "Game of Thrones."

14.2 Tonicizing the Dominant

The perfect fifth is one of the most foundational intervals in music. Acoustically, it is the most basic interval after the octave. Key signatures that are related by fifth are very closely related, differing only by a single sharp or flat. Accordingly, changing key from the tonic to the dominant (up by fifth) is extremely common, especially in the common practice period of western art music. In the rest of this chapter, we will explore motion from the tonic to the dominant. In this section, we will focus on tonicizing the dominant.

Tonicizing the Dominant in Major

In major, we can tonicize the dominant by raising the fourth degree of the scale. The raised fourth degree acts as the leading tone to five.

Tonicizing V in Major Vocalise

14.2a

28 Deutsche Volkslieder, WoO 32 - No. 1, Die Schnürbrust

Johannes Brahms

14.2b

Kinderszenen, Op. 15 - No. 2, Curiose Geschichte

Robert Schumann

14.2c

Lied des Orpheus, als er in die Hölle ging., D. 474

Franz Schubert

14.2d

Tonicizing the Dominant in Minor

Tonicizing the dominant in minor can be slightly more complex than in major, because of the chromatic variations available in the minor scale. Sometimes the dominant chord in minor is a major chord; sometimes it is a minor chord, depending on whether the seventh degree of the scale is raised or not. Either way, the dominant is generally tonicized by raising the fourth and/or sixth scale degrees.

Tonicizing v in Minor Vocalise

14.2e

28 Deutsche Volkslieder - Auf, gebet uns das Pfingstei

Johannes Brahms

14.2f

La Forza del Destino - Overture

Giuseppe Verdi

14.2g

Kinderszenen, Op. 15 - No. 10, Fast zu ernst

Robert Schumann

14.2. TONICIZING THE DOMINANT

14.2h
Gavotte, Op. 23

Camille Saint-Saëns

Mixed Examples

14.2i
Piano Concerto No. 24 in C minor, K. 491

Wolfgang Amadeus Mozart

14.2j
Ma fin est mon commencement

Guillaume de Machaut

14.2k
Variationen über ein Thema von Robert Schumann
Clara Schumann

14.2l
Flute Sonata in A minor, HWV 374
George Frideric Handel

14.2. TONICIZING THE DOMINANT

14.2m

Pallade e Marte - Sinfonia
Maria Margherita Grimani

Specialty Examples

14.2n Canon

13 Canons, Op. 113 - Göttlicher Morpheus
Johannes Brahms

14.2o Jam Session

14.2p Analysis

14.2. TONICIZING THE DOMINANT

14.2q Figured Bass

14.2r Lead Sheet

14.2s Find the Music

14.2t Fill in the Blanks

14.2. TONICIZING THE DOMINANT

Listening Examples

- Anthem: John Stafford Smith and Francis Scott Key, "The Star-Spangled Banner."

- Standard: Billy Strayhorn, "Take the 'A' Train." Focus on the second half of the bridge.

- Musical Theater: Richard Rodgers and Oscar Hammerstein II, "Do Re Mi," from *The Sound of Music* (original cast recording, 0:42–1:15).

- Television: Earle Hagen and Herbert W. Spencer, theme from "The Andy Griffith Show."

- Rock: The Beatles, "Maxwell's Silver Hammer," from *Abbey Road* (0:00–0:51), written by John Lennon and Paul McCartney.

14.3 Modulating to the Dominant

In this section, I want you to practice shifting your orientation from one key to another. At the "New" indication, start treating $\hat{5}$ as the new $\hat{1}$. If you are using movable do solfege, treat "sol" as the new "do" (or "mi" as the new "la" for la-minor). At the "Init." indication, where applicable, shift your orientation back to the initial key. Though many of these examples are short enough that you could stay in the initial key throughout, the point is to practice shifting and shifting back. This practice will serve you when you encounter longer modulations in other music that you study.

Modulating to the Dominant in Major

14.3a

Tyroler Sind Lustig

Jakob Haibel

14.3. MODULATING TO THE DOMINANT

14.3b

Kuss-Walzer, Op. 400

Johann Strauss II

14.3c

Nocturne in B flat major

Maria Agata Szymanowska

14.3d

Nabucco - Chorus of the Hebrew Slaves

Giuseppe Verdi

Modulating to the Dominant in Minor

14.3e

Violin Concerto No. 3 in B minor, Op. 61

Camille Saint-Saëns

14.3. MODULATING TO THE DOMINANT

14.3f
Swung (♩ = 116)

14.3g
Malinconico (♩. = 54)

14.3h

Piano Sonata No. 11 in A major, K. 331/300i

Wolfgang Amadeus Mozart

Mixed Examples

Here, I no longer indicate "New" or "Init." Study each example. Where do the accidentals imply a shift to $\hat{5}$ or a shift from $\hat{5}$ back to $\hat{1}$? Decide for yourself where to shift and where, when appropriate, to shift back.

14.3i

Auf der Alma

Traditional

14.3. MODULATING TO THE DOMINANT

14.3j

Prelude in F sharp minor, BWV 883

Johann Sebastian Bach

14.3k

Piano Sonata No. 10 in C Major, K. 330

Wolfgang Amadeus Mozart

14.3l

Peer Gynt Suite No. 1, Op. 46 - Anitra's Dance

Edvard Grieg

14.3. MODULATING TO THE DOMINANT

14.3m

Recorder Sonata, TWV 41:F2
Georg Phillip Telemann

Specialty Examples

14.3n Trio

Prelude in E major, BWV 854

Johann Sebastian Bach

14.3. MODULATING TO THE DOMINANT

14.3o Jam Session

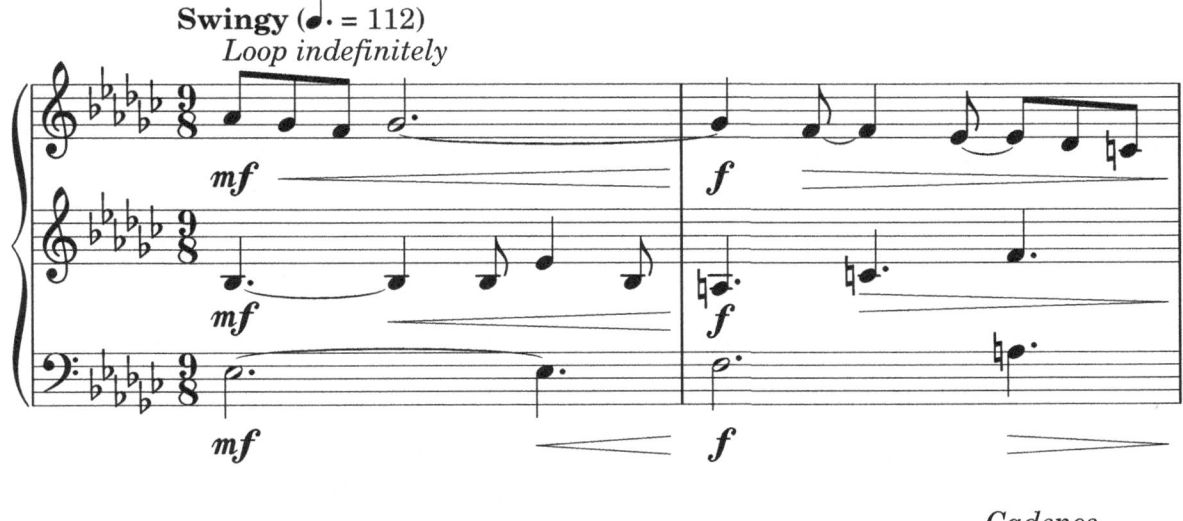

14.3p Analysis

14.3q Figured Bass

14.3. MODULATING TO THE DOMINANT

14.3r Lead Sheet

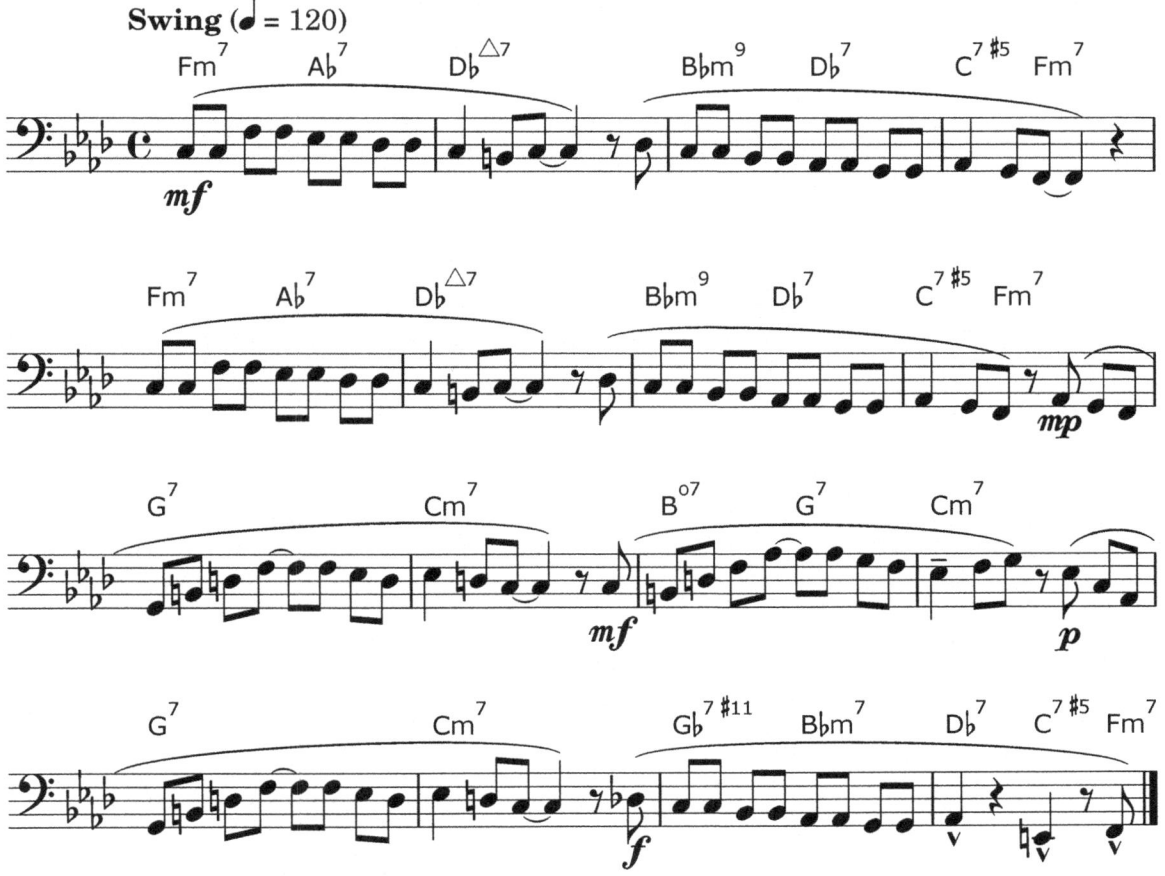

14.3s Find the Music

14.3t Fill in the Blanks

Listening Examples

- Classical: Johann Sebastian Bach, 15 Inventions - No. 1, Invention in C Major, BWV 772. This piece is in common time with steady sixteenth notes. Try transcribing the first six bars, ending on the downbeat of bar seven.

- Classical: Johann Sebastian Bach, *Well-Tempered Clavier*, Book I - Prelude No. 1 in C major, BWV 846. This piece is also in common time with steady sixteenth notes. Try transcribing the first eleven bars.

- Classical: Wolfgang Amadeus Mozart, Piano Sonata No. 16 in C Major, K. 545. The first half of this piece modulates from I to V.

- Country: Dolly Parton, "Highlight of My Life," from *Jolene*.

- Alternative: Fiona Apple, "Shadowboxer," from *Tidal* (0:00–1:40).

14.4 More Movement to the Dominant

The examples in this section mix tonicization and modulation. You may want to keep your orientation to the initial key. You may want to shift your orientation to the key of the dominant. Study each example carefully and decide how best to approach it based on your experience from Sections 2 and 3.

Major Key Examples

14.4a

Cello Sonata, Op. 46

Louise Farrenc

CHAPTER 14. BASIC KEY RELATIONSHIPS

14.4b

Symphony No. 3, Op. 55 - III

Ludwig van Beethoven

14.4c

La gazza ladra - Overture

Gioacchino Rossini

14.4. MORE MOVEMENT TO THE DOMINANT

14.4d

Sonata in A major, Op. 1 - No. 5

Muzio Clementi

Minor Key Examples

14.4e

Sonate für Pianoforte und Violoncell

Johannes Brahms

14.4f

Fugue in B minor, BWV 869

Johann Sebastian Bach

14.4. MORE MOVEMENT TO THE DOMINANT

14.4g

Salve Regina
Giovanni Battista Pergolesi

14.4h

Sinfonia in F minor, BWV 794
Johann Sebastian Bach

Mixed Examples

14.4i

Bal masqué, Op. 22

Amy Beach

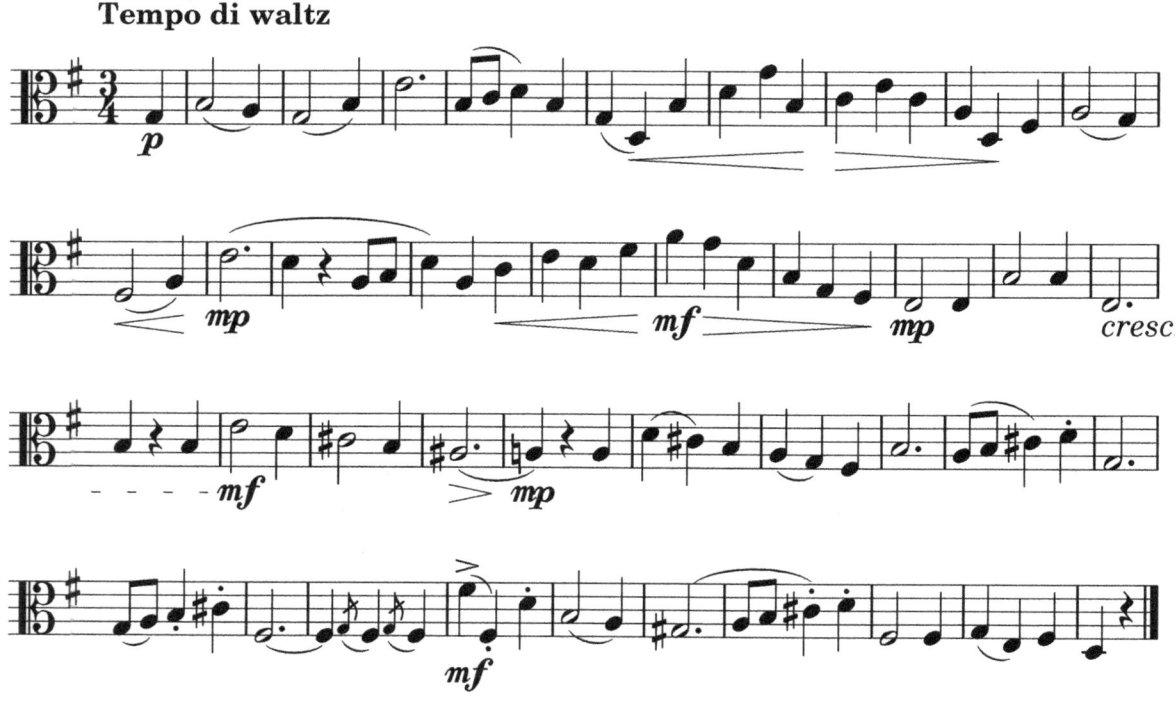

14.4j

Lied eines Kriegers, D. 822

Franz Schubert

14.4. MORE MOVEMENT TO THE DOMINANT

14.4k

Symphony No. 9 in D minor, Op. 125

Ludwig van Beethoven

14.4l

Cello Concerto in C major, G. 477

Luigi Boccherini

14.4m

Prelude in A minor, BWV 889

Johann Sebastian Bach

14.4. MORE MOVEMENT TO THE DOMINANT

Specialty Examples

14.4n Duet

Invention in C minor, BWV 773

Johann Sebastian Bach

14.4o Jam Session

14.4. MORE MOVEMENT TO THE DOMINANT

14.4p Analysis

14.4q Figured Bass

14.4. MORE MOVEMENT TO THE DOMINANT

14.4r Lead Sheet

14.4s Find the Music

14.4t Fill in the Blanks

Listening Examples

- Standard: Richard Rodgers and Lorenz Hart, "I Could Write a Book."

- Rock: The Beatles, "Michelle," from *Rubber Soul*, written by John Lennon and Paul McCartney.

- Folk Rock: Bob Dylan, "You're Gonna Make Me Lonesome When You Go," from *Blood on the Tracks*.

- Pop: Barbra Streisand, "People," from *People*, written by Bob Merrill and Jule Styne.

- Musical Theater: Claude-Michel Schönberg, Jean-Claude Lucchetti Mourou, Herbert Kretzmer, and Alain Boublil, "Do You Hear the People Sing," from *Les Misérables*.

Chapter 15

Changing Meters

In this chapter, we will explore rhythms with meter changes. The most basic kinds of meter changes involve changing like meters: staying in simple or in compound throughout while changing the number of beats in the bar. Changing from 4/4 to 3/4 meter or from 12/8 to 9/8 are examples of changing like meters. We will work with changing like meters in Section 1.

More complicated meter changes mix simple and compound meters. There are two ways to do this: by keeping the division constant or keeping the beat constant. We will explore both techniques in Sections 2 and 3.

We can think of the overall organization of meter in a rhythm as the "meter structure." While learning an example, it is often helpful to study the meter structure. Do the meter changes follow predictable patterns? Do they happen at the ends of phrases or within phrases? Try writing out the meter structure by representing each bar of a rhythm with the numerator of its time signature, indicating 2-2-3-3 for two bars of 2/4 followed by two bars of 3/4 or 6-6-9-9-9 for two bars of 6/8 followed by three bars of 9/8. You may also find it useful to practice scanning the rhythm while counting, scanning while conducting, and clapping on the downbeat of every bar while performing the rhythm.

15.1 Changing Like Meters

In this section, we will explore changing between duple, triple, and quadruple meters within a single example. The length of the beat will not change, but the number of beats in a bar will. The result is that some bars will be longer than others.

Give particular attention to the downbeat of each bar. If you can clearly feel each downbeat, it will help you stay oriented. If you can accentuate the downbeat in your performance, it will help the listener stay oriented too.

15.1a

15.1b

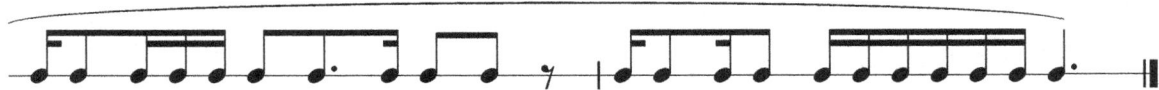

15.1c Interpret

Très vif (♪ = 126)

15.1d Interpret

With painstaking precision (♪. = 60)

15.1e

With fire (♩ = 120)

15.1f

Espressivo (♩. = 72)

15.1. CHANGING LIKE METERS

15.1g

Vigorously (♩ = 116)

15.1h

15.1. CHANGING LIKE METERS

15.1i

15.1j

Tempo semplice (♩. = 54)

15.2 Mixing Simple and Compound with a Constant Division

Count aloud in steady time: "1-2-1-2-1-2..." Now, count "1-2-3-1-2-3..." Go back and forth between "1-2" and "1-2-3" without changing the speed of your counting. Once you get the hang of this, start clapping on every "1." Your claps should be closer together when counting "1-2" and farther apart when counting "1-2-3."

This is the feel of switching between simple and compound meter with a constant division. You are clapping the beat and counting the division. As you have noticed, the length of the beat will change, being shorter in simple meter and longer in compound meter. The length of the division will not change, with two divisions per beat in simple meter and three per beat in compound.

Notice that the tempo text for these examples indicates that the division is constant.

15.2a

15.2b

Sonoro, eighth constant (♩ = 80)

15.2c Interpret

Andante, eighth constant (♩ = 88)

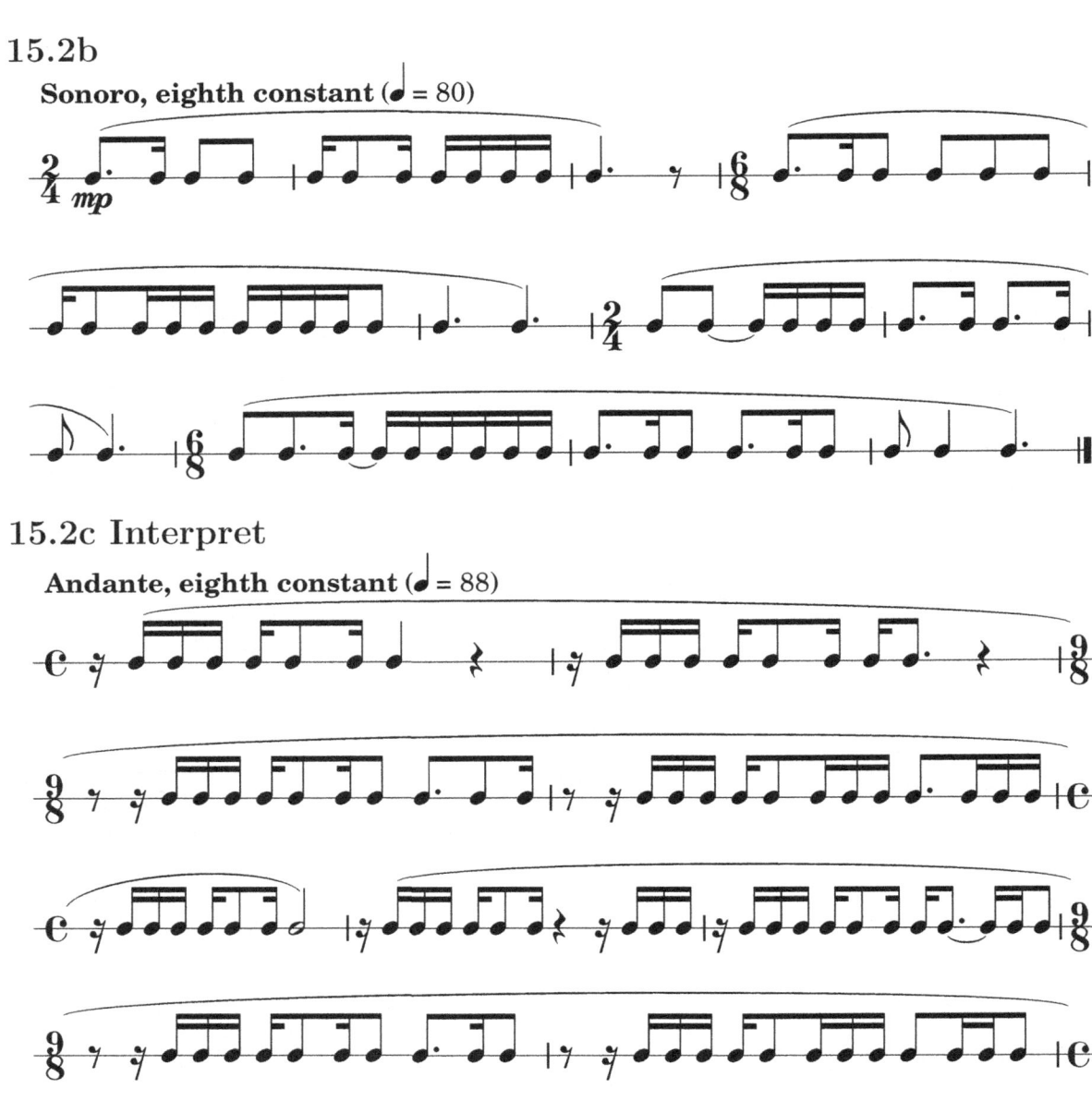

15.2d Interpret

Mirror images, quarter constant ($\dot{} = 72$)

15.2e

Spiritoso, eighth constant ($\dot{}\cdot = 132$)

15.2f

Merrily, sixteenth constant ($\flat\cdot$ = 76)

15.2g

Energico, eighth constant ($\quarternote\cdot$ = 69)

15.2. MIXING SIMPLE AND COMPOUND WITH A CONSTANT DIVISION 99

15.2h

Whimsically ambling, eighth constant ($\quarternote. = 80$)

15.2i

Rebelliously, quarter constant ($\half = 76$)

15.2. MIXING SIMPLE AND COMPOUND WITH A CONSTANT DIVISION

15.2j

Deciso, eighth constant ($\eighthnote = 96$)

15.3 Mixing Simple and Compound with a Constant Beat

In this section, we will change between simple and compound meter while preserving a constant beat. Notice that the metronome mark for each example indicates that the beat in simple meter equals the beat in compound meter. When switching from simple to compound, try feeling the compound material as if it were written with triplets. When switching from compound to simple, try feeling the simple material as if it were written with duplets and quadruplets.

15.3c Interpret

15.3d Interpret

15.3. MIXING SIMPLE AND COMPOUND WITH A CONSTANT BEAT

15.3g

15.3h

Laid back groove ($\quarter = \dottedquarter = 63$)

15.3. MIXING SIMPLE AND COMPOUND WITH A CONSTANT BEAT

15.3i

15.3j

15.3. MIXING SIMPLE AND COMPOUND WITH A CONSTANT BEAT

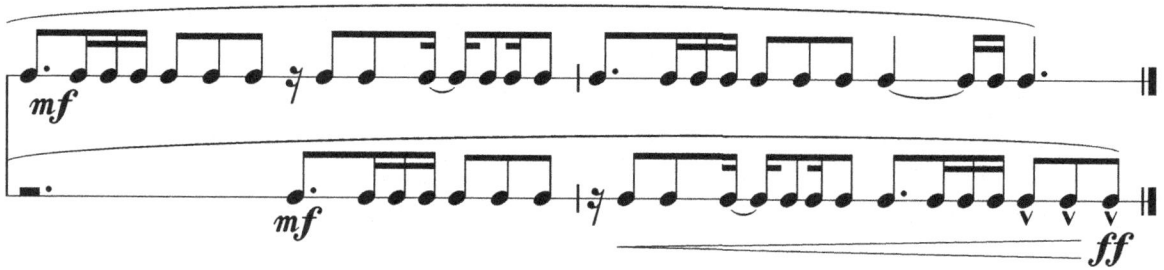

Chapter 16

More Key Relationships

In Chapter 14, we began to connect melodic material from two different key areas, working with the most common key relationships. In this chapter, we will continue this exploration, working with more distant key relationships. In Sections 1 and 2, we will explore tonicizing and modulating to the subdominant. In Section 3, we will explore moving to the supertonic and mediant key areas in major. In Section 4, we will work with moving to the submediant and subtonic key areas in minor, introducing the Neapolitan chord along the way.

16.1 Tonicizing the Subdominant

Just as it is common to tonicize the dominant, a fifth above the tonic, it is also common to tonicize the subdominant, a fifth below the tonic.

Major Key Examples

In major, the subdominant is generally tonicized by lowering the seventh degree of the scale. This creates a dominant seventh on the tonic of the scale: V7 of IV.

Tonicizing IV Vocalise

16.1a

Prelude in C major, BWV 870

Johann Sebastian Bach

16.1b

Prelude in E flat major, BWV 853

Johann Sebastian Bach

16.1. TONICIZING THE SUBDOMINANT

16.1c

16.1d

Eine Nacht in Venedig

Johann Strauss II

Minor Key Examples

In minor, the subdominant is often tonicized by raising the third degree of the scale, which acts as a leading tone to iv. When iv is tonicized with a diminished seventh chord a lowered second degree is also used, as demonstrated in bar three of the vocalise below.

16.1g

Piano Concerto No. 3 in D minor, Op. 30

Sergei Rachmaninoff

16.1h

Semelé

Élisabeth Jacquet de La Guerre

Mixed Examples

16.1i

Invention in G major, BWV 781

Johann Sebastian Bach

16.1. TONICIZING THE SUBDOMINANT

16.1j

Symphony No. 8 in F major, Op. 93

Ludwig van Beethoven

16.1k

Invention in A minor, BWV 784

Johann Sebastian Bach

16.1l

Piano Trio in D minor, Op. 11

Fanny Mendelssohn

16.1. TONICIZING THE SUBDOMINANT

16.1m

Prelude in C major, BWV 846

Johann Sebastian Bach

Specialty Examples

16.1n Trio

Missa Prima, Op. 18 - Credo (Crucifixus)

Isabella Leonarda

16.1. TONICIZING THE SUBDOMINANT

16.1o Jam Session

Magnifico (♩. = 112)
Loop indefinitely

16.1p Analysis

16.1. TONICIZING THE SUBDOMINANT

16.1q Figured Bass

16.1r Lead Sheet

16.1s Find the Music

16.1t Fill in the Blanks

16.1. TONICIZING THE SUBDOMINANT

Listening Examples

- Musical Theater: Jerry Bock and Sheldon Harnick, "Sunrise, Sunset," from *Fiddler on the Roof* (original cast recording, 0:06–0:48).

- Jazz: Oliver Nelson, "Cascades," from *The Blues and the Abstract Truth* (0:04–0:36). Focus on the saxophone melody.

- Standard: Luiz Bonfá and Antônio Maria, "Manhã de Carnaval (Theme from Black Orpheus)."

- Rock: The Beatles, "Hey Jude," from *Past Masters*, written by John Lennon and Paul McCartney. The shift to IV first comes at the fifty-three second mark.

- Psychedelic Rock: The Beatles, "Lucy in the Sky with Diamonds," from *Sgt. Pepper's Lonely Hearts Club Band* (0:00–0:33), written by John Lennon and Paul McCartney. Learn the opening instrumental part along with the vocal melody as a two-part texture.

- Rock: The Beatles, "You Never Give Me Your Money," from *Abbey Road* (1:10–1:49), written by John Lennon and Paul McCartney. The flat seventh here is used two ways: as part of a V7 of IV and as a part of the genuine Mixolydian sound. We will discuss Mixolydian in chapter 18.

- Rock: The Beatles, "Something," from *Abbey Road* (0:05–0:39), written by George Harrison.

- Country: Emmylou Harris, "Even Cowgirls Get the Blues," from *Blue Kentucky Girl*, written by Rodney Crowell.

- Video Games: Lorne Balfe and Jesper Kyd, "Assassin's Creed: Revelations," performed by The London Philharmonic Orchestra, from *The Greatest Video Game Music 2* (0:00–1:23). Hear this in a slow common time. The move from G minor to C minor occurs mostly in the harmonies, but notice how the vocal part draws on the leading tone of each key.

16.2 Modulating to the Subdominant

In this section, we explore modulating to the subdominant. Practice changing your orientation in the middle of each example so that you are thinking in terms of a new key, with the subdominant as the new tonic. Though it would be possible to think of each example only in the context of the initial key, do not do this. The goal is to build the skill of shifting your orientation from one key to another. Having grounded the initial key in your ear, you need to be able to shift your perspective quickly to hear materials in the context of a new key while maintaining enough aural connection to the original key to safely find your way back again. This skill will serve you when you encounter longer modulations in other music that you study. For Examples A through H, I use "New" and "Init." to indicate where to shift to the new key and where to return to the initial key.

Major Key Examples

16.2a
La Traviata - Coro di Zingarelle (Chorus of Gypsies)

Giuseppe Verdi

16.2b

16.2. MODULATING TO THE SUBDOMINANT

16.2c

16.2d

Caprises en forme de Valse, Op. 2

Clara Schumann

Minor Key Examples

16.2e

16.2. MODULATING TO THE SUBDOMINANT

16.2f

16.2g

Violin Concerto No. 8 in A minor, Op. 47

Louis Spohr

16.2h

Prelude in G minor, BWV 885

Johann Sebastian Bach

16.2. MODULATING TO THE SUBDOMINANT

Mixed Examples

Some of these examples modulate to the subdominant while others only tonicize the subdominant. Some move right away to the key area of the subdominant while others take time to establish the key area of the tonic. Some also tonicize the dominant while others do not. Use your discernment here. Study each example carefully and decide how best to approach it.

16.2i

Ego sum resurrectio

José Maurício Nunes Garcia

16.2j

Prelude in C minor, BWV 847

Johann Sebastian Bach

16.2k

Symphony No. 2 in D major, Op. 36

Ludwig van Beethoven

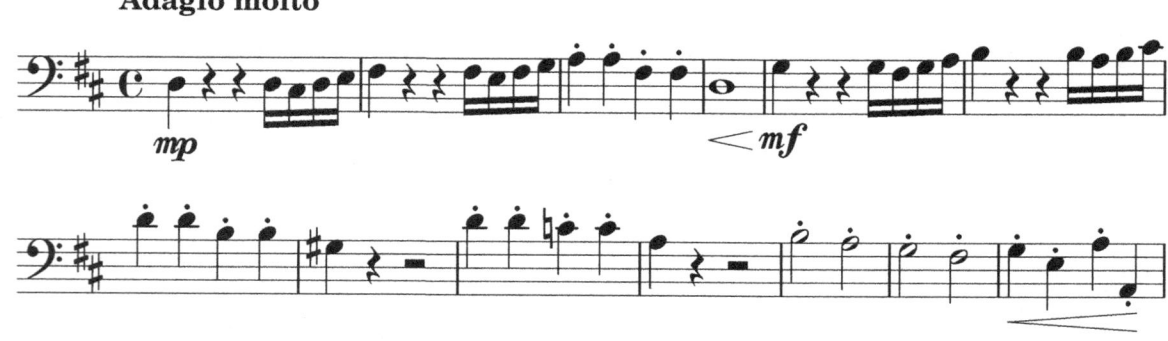

16.2. MODULATING TO THE SUBDOMINANT

16.2l

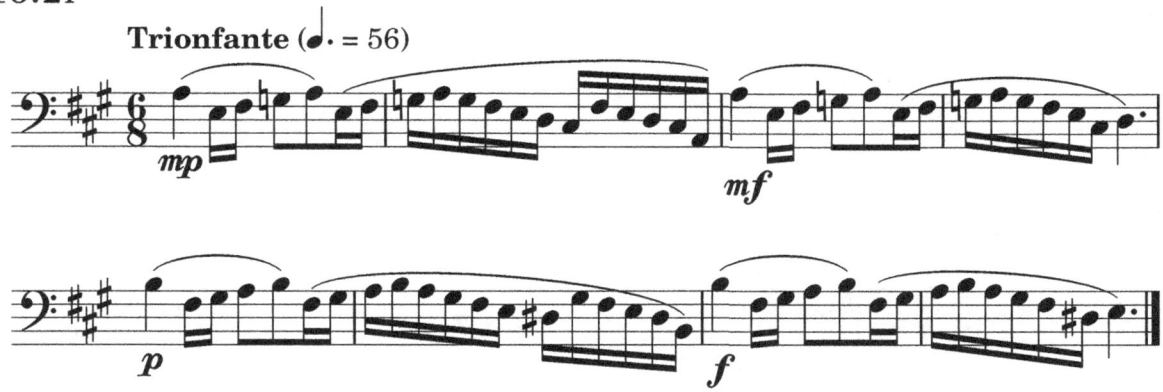

16.2m

Recorder Sonata in D minor, TWV 41:d4

Georg Philipp Telemann

Specialty Examples

16.2n Duet

16.2. MODULATING TO THE SUBDOMINANT

16.2o Jam Session

Pleasant ambling ($\quarternote = 92$)
Loop indefinitely

16.2p Analysis

16.2q Figured Bass

16.2. MODULATING TO THE SUBDOMINANT

16.2r Lead Sheet

16.2s Find the Music

16.2t Fill in the Blanks

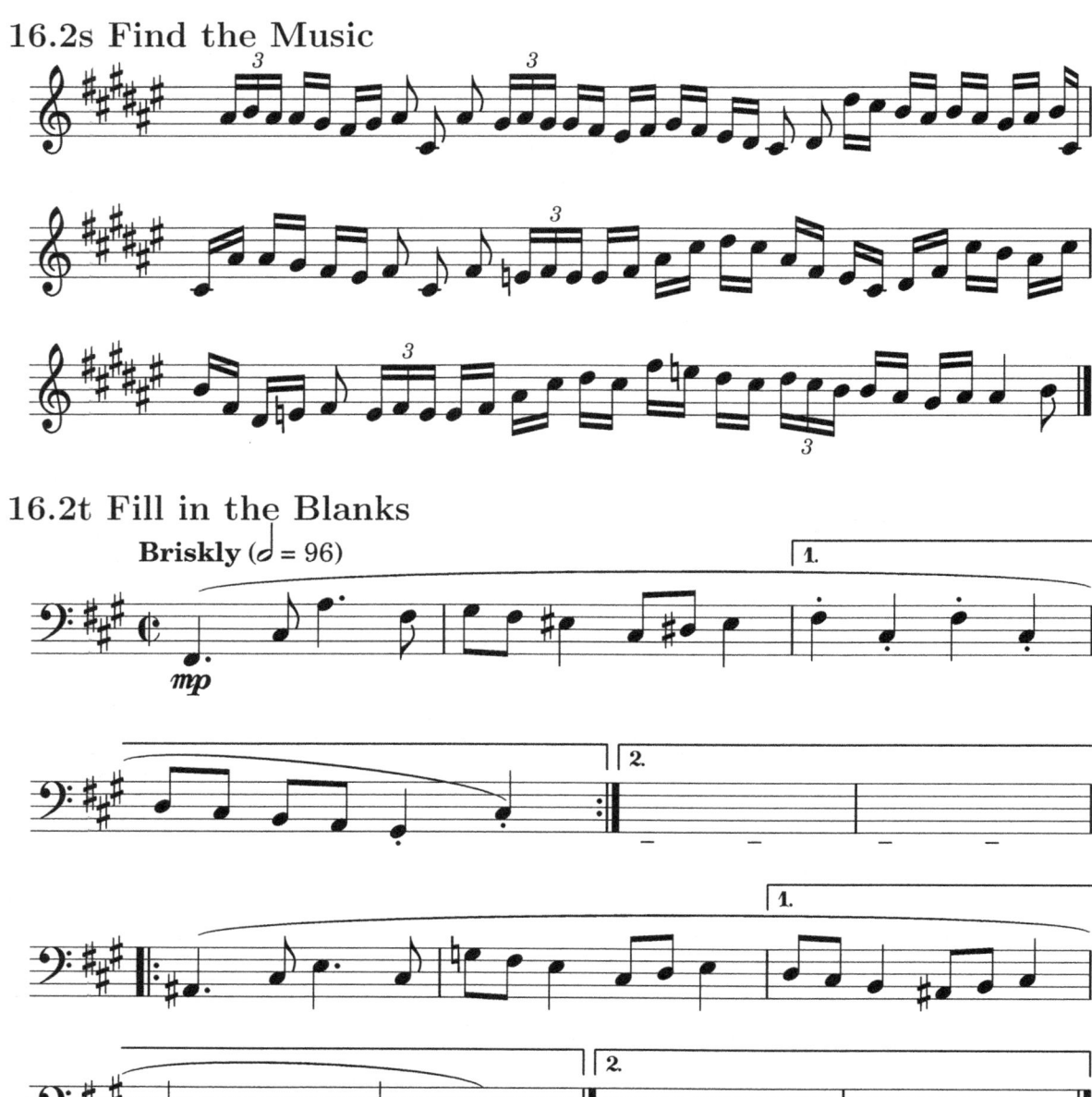

16.2. MODULATING TO THE SUBDOMINANT

Listening Examples

- Jazz: Jelly Roll Morton, "The Pearls," from *The Jazz Piano Collection*. The move to IV happens around the two and a half minute mark.

- Standard: Bob Haggart and Johnny Burke, "What's New." The A section features a great parallel major/minor relationship and the bridge modulates to IV.

- Standard: Edgar Battle and Eddie Durham, "Topsy."

- Musical Theater: Cole Porter, "Where is the Life that Late I Led," from *Kiss Me, Kate* (original cast recording, 0:08–1:09).

- Musical Theater: Meredith Willson, "76 Trombones," from *The Music Man* (original cast recording, 1:12–2:12).

- Standard: Sonny Rollins, "Pent-Up House."

- Rock: The Beatles, "Sgt. Pepper's Lonely Hearts Club Band," from *Sgt. Pepper's Lonely Hearts Club Band*, written by John Lennon and Paul McCartney. The move to IV comes at 1:37 when the brass first enters.

- Rock: The Beatles, "I Want You (She's so Heavy)," from *Abbey Road* (0:13–0:55), written by John Lennon and Paul McCartney.

- Indie Rock: Regina Spektor, "Fidelity," from *Begin to Hope*. I hear this song as beginning in C and moving to F very quickly. Though F turns out to be the primary key, without returning to C until after the two minute mark, the opening has all the feel of a move from I to IV.

16.3 Secondary Key Relationships in Major

Think of the tonic, dominant, and subdominant as the primary triads of a key. This leaves the mediant, submediant, supertonic, and subtonic/leading tone as the secondary triads of the key. We have amply explored moving to the key areas of the dominant (in Chapter 14) and subdominant (in the first two sections of this chapter). We now continue our exploration of connecting closely related keys by moving to the key areas of the secondary triads. We will work with the key areas of secondary triads in major keys in this section and minor keys in the next.

In major, the secondary triads are ii, iii, vi, and vii°. We explored moving to vi in Chapter 14 when we worked with relative major/minor. As vii° is an unstable triad, being diminished, it does not represent a stable key area without alteration. We shall focus here, therefore, on moving to ii and iii.

When you orient to the initial major key here, make a point of orienting to the relative minor as well. This is useful because the secondary chords in major are the primary chords of the relative minor (ii and iii in major are iv and v of the relative minor). Our previous work moving to iv and v in minor should form the foundation for moving to ii and iii in major.

Moving to ii

The supertonic in major, ii, is most often tonicized by raising the first scale degree, as modeled in the vocalise below.

Tonicizing ii Vocalise

16.3a

Symphony No. 8 in B minor, D. 759 (Unfinished)

Franz Schubert

16.3. SECONDARY KEY RELATIONSHIPS IN MAJOR

16.3b

Maple Leaf Rag

Scott Joplin

16.3c

Vier Lieder für das Pianoforte, Op. 2

Fanny Mendelssohn

16.3d

Italian Sketches for Piano, Op. 33 - No. 1, Venise

Teresa Carreño

Moving to iii

The mediant in major, iii, is most often tonicized by raising the second and fourth scale degrees as illustrated in the vocalise below.

Tonicizing iii Vocalise

16.3e

16.3. SECONDARY KEY RELATIONSHIPS IN MAJOR

16.3f

The Thriller Rag

May Frances Aufderheide

16.3g

Sechs Lieder, Op. 13 - Ich Stand in Dunklen Träumen

Clara Schumann

16.3h

Kinderszenen, Op. 15 - No. 4, Bittendes Kind

Robert Schumann

16.3. SECONDARY KEY RELATIONSHIPS IN MAJOR

Mixed Examples

16.3i

String Quartet No. 3 in D major, Op. 18

Ludwig van Beethoven

16.3j

Soirées Musicales, Op. 6 - No. 1, Toccatina

Clara Schumann

16.3k

Leola

Scott Joplin

16.3. SECONDARY KEY RELATIONSHIPS IN MAJOR

16.3l

Eugenia

Scott Joplin

16.3m

Oboe Sonata in B flat major, TWV 41:B6

Georg Philipp Telemann

Specialty Examples

16.3n Duet

16.3. SECONDARY KEY RELATIONSHIPS IN MAJOR

16.3o Jam Session

16.3p Analysis

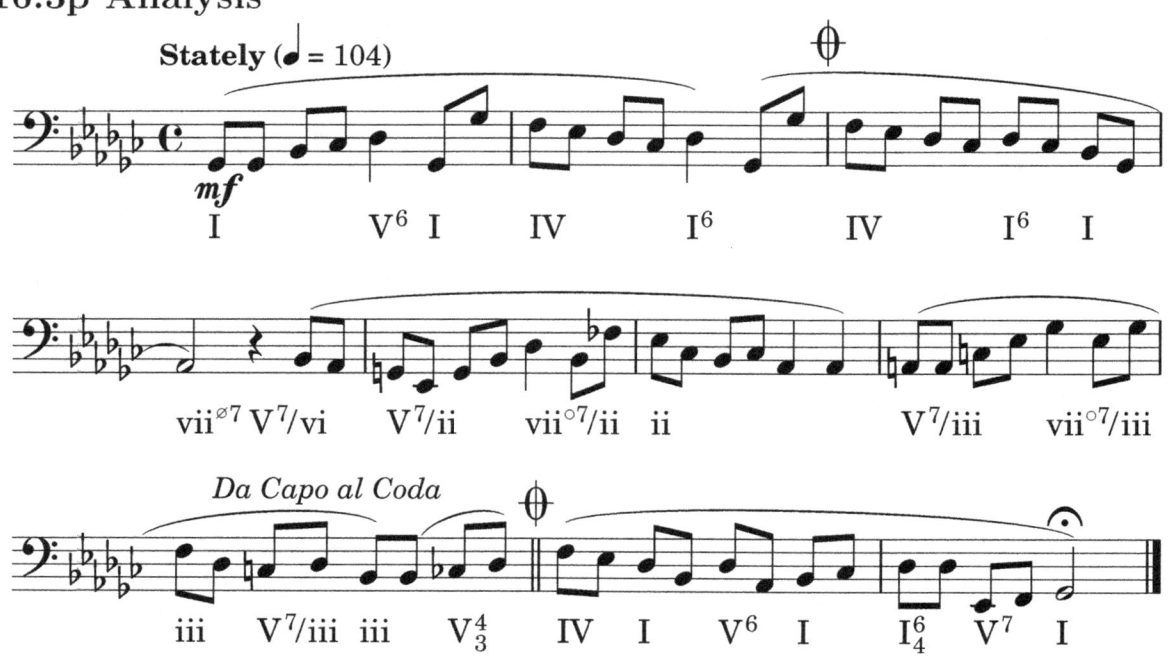

16.3q Figured Bass

16.3. SECONDARY KEY RELATIONSHIPS IN MAJOR

16.3r Lead Sheet

16.3s Find the Music

16.3t Fill in the Blanks

Listening Examples

- Musical Theater: Richard Rodgers and Oscar Hammerstein II, "Oklahoma," from *Oklahoma* (original cast recording, 0:04–0:54).

- Television: Dale Evans, theme from "Happy Trails."

- Television: Vic Mizzy, theme from "The Addams Family."

- Standard: Miles Davis, "The Serpent's Tooth."

- Musical Theater: Leonard Bernstein and Stephen Sondheim, "Tonight," from *West Side Story* (original cast recording, 0:05–0:48).

- Standard: Willie Nelson, "Crazy."

- R&B: Stevie Wonder, "I Just Called to Say I Love You," from *The Woman in Red*.

16.4 Secondary Key Relationships in Minor

The secondary triads in minor are ii°, III, VI, VII, and vii°. We have already worked with moving to III in Chapter 14 when we worked with relative major/minor key relationships. As ii° and vii° are unstable, being diminished, we will not work with them as destinations for tonicization and modulation. A common alteration of the supertonic in minor, the Neapolitan, does bear exploring though. The Neapolitan, ♭II, is created by lowering the second degree of the minor scale, yielding a major supertonic triad. We shall thus focus in this section on the key areas of VI, VII, and ♭II.

Moving to VI

When orienting to the initial minor key, be sure to orient to the relative major as well. This is useful because VI in minor is IV in the key of the relative major, and moving to IV in major is already familiar from our work in the first half of this chapter.

Tonicizing VI Vocalise

16.4a

16.4b

Lied der Anne Lyle, D. 830
Franz Schubert

16.4c

Prelude in E flat minor, BWV 876
Johann Sebastian Bach

16.4. SECONDARY KEY RELATIONSHIPS IN MINOR

16.4d

Symphony No. 2 in D major, Op. 36

Ludwig van Beethoven

Moving to VII

As above, be sure to orient to the key area of the relative major. Moving to VII in minor is analogous to moving to V in the key of the relative major.

Tonicizing VII Vocalise

16.4e

16.4. SECONDARY KEY RELATIONSHIPS IN MINOR

16.4f

Oboe Sonata in A minor, TWV 41:a3
Georg Philipp Telemann

16.4g

16.4h

Concerto Grosso in B minor, Op. 6
George Frideric Handel

16.4. SECONDARY KEY RELATIONSHIPS IN MINOR

The Neapolitan

Another common extension of the minor key is the Neapolitan chord: the major triad built on the lowered second degree of the minor scale. The following examples introduce the sound of the Neapolitan. The Grieg example touches on the Neapolitan only briefly; the Mozart, Chopin, and Rossini examples linger a little longer; the Hensel presents the Neapolitan in the context of the parallel major key. Look for the lowered second degree of the scale; that's the hallmark of the Neapolitan sound.

Neapolitan Vocalise

16.4i

Piano Concerto in A minor, Op. 16

Edvard Grieg

16.4j

Piano Concerto No. 23 in A major, K. 488

Wolfgang Amadeus Mozart

16.4k

Polonaises, Op. 26 - Polonaise No. 1 in C sharp minor

Frédéric Chopin

16.4. SECONDARY KEY RELATIONSHIPS IN MINOR

16.4l

3 Mélodies, Op. 5

Fanny Mendelssohn Hensel

16.4m

La Danza (Tarantella)

Gioacchino Rossini

Specialty Examples

16.4n Canon

13 Canons, Op. 113 - No. 12, Rückert

Johannes Brahms

16.4o Jam Session

16.4. SECONDARY KEY RELATIONSHIPS IN MINOR

16.4p Analysis

16.4q Figured Bass

16.4. SECONDARY KEY RELATIONSHIPS IN MINOR

16.4r Lead Sheet

16.4s Find the Music

16.4t Fill in the Blanks

16.4. SECONDARY KEY RELATIONSHIPS IN MINOR

Listening Examples

- Classical: Ludwig van Beethoven, Piano Sonata No. 14, "Moonlight" (first movement). Focus on the right hand arpeggio in the opening eight bars. Can you find the Neapolitan chord?

- Classical: Frédéric Chopin, Prelude No. 6 in B minor, Op. 28.

- Musical Theater: Richard Adler and Jerry Ross, "Whatever Lola Wants," from *Damn Yankees* (original cast recording, 0:04–1:17).

- Rock: The Beatles, "Because," from *Abbey Road* (0:00–0:55), written by John Lennon and Paul McCartney. Focus on the arpeggios in the guitar here.

- Standard: Kenny Dorham, "Blue Bossa." Bars 9-12 are in the key of the Neapolitan.

- Neo Soul: Alicia Keys, "Piano & I," from *Songs in A Minor*, written by Alicia Keys and Ludwig Van Beethoven. Here is a modern remix of the opening of Beethoven's Moonlight Sonata. Enjoy the Neapolitan at the twenty-three second mark — contains explicit lyrics.

Chapter 17

Odd and Composite Meters

Thus far, all of the meters we have used have had certain properties. They have had either two, three, or four beats, and all of the beats within a single bar have been the same length. The concept of meter is actually more flexible than this though. Meters can have five beats, or seven. We call these "odd meters," because their numerators are odd.

The beats within a meter also do not need to be the same length. Consider a bar with eight eighth notes. These could be organized as four groups of two, as in 4/4. But suppose that the eighth notes are consistently grouped as 3 + 3 + 2. Rather than writing the rhythm in 4/4 with lots of accents and irregular beaming, the composer can express the consistent 3 + 3 + 2 grouping more directly by writing the meter as 3+3+2/8. Think of this meter as a composite of compound and simple meters. The first two beats are compound beats, having three divisions, and the last beat is a simple beat, having two divisions. The division is constant throughout. Meters with unequal beats like this are known as "composite meters."

17.1 Quintuple and Septuple Meters

Our first three examples are in 5/4 meter. The five beats of 5/4 generally break down into three beats plus two beats (strong-weak-weak-strong-weak) or two beats plus three beats (strong-weak-strong-weak-weak). Study each rhythm to get a sense of how the bar is divided. Let your conducting pattern reflect the breakdown of the meter: three beats plus two would be down-in-in-out-up and two plus three would be down-in-out-out-up.

17.1a

17.1b

17.1. QUINTUPLE AND SEPTUPLE METERS

17.1c Interpret

Chill (♩ = 92)

The next three examples are in 7/4. Again, study each rhythm. Do you feel the seven as four plus three or as three plus four? The easiest way to conduct a bar of seven would be to combine a four pattern with a 3 pattern with the second pattern higher and smaller than the first: down-in-out-up plus a higher and smaller down-out-up (four plus three), or down-out-up plus a higher and smaller down-in-out-up (three plus four).

17.1d Interpret

Swing (♩ = 126)

17.1e

Affettuoso (♩ = 132)

17.1. QUINTUPLE AND SEPTUPLE METERS

17.1f

Leggiadro (♩ = 84)

17.1g

17.1. QUINTUPLE AND SEPTUPLE METERS

17.1h

17.1i

17.1. QUINTUPLE AND SEPTUPLE METERS

17.1j

17.2 Composite Meters

The examples in this section feature meters with uneven beats. These meters are sometimes referred to as "composite," "asymmetric," "unequal," or "mixed" meters. Think of this as mixing beats from simple and compound meters within a single bar. Some beats have two divisions (simple) while other beats have three (compound). The division of the beat is always constant.

In most of these examples, the numerator of the meter represents the groupings of the divisions into beats. When this is not the case (as in examples H and I), you can figure out how the divisions are grouped by studying how the notes are beamed. When conducting, adapt duple, triple, or quadruple beat patterns with longer and shorter beats as needed. For beats with two divisions, use simple meter syllables. For beats with three divisions, use compound meter syllables.

Syllables in Composite Meters

17.2a

17.2. COMPOSITE METERS

17.2b
Tempestuously ($\dot{\ }$. = 104)

17.2c Interpret
Dancelike ($\dot{\ }$ = 116)

17.2d Interpret

Ecstatically (♩ = 168)

17.2e

Giocoso (♩. = 84)

17.2. COMPOSITE METERS

17.2f

17.2g

17.2. COMPOSITE METERS

17.2h

17.2i

17.2. COMPOSITE METERS

17.2j

17.3 Changing Composite Meters

The examples in this section feature meter changes with uneven beats. The duration of any particular note value will remain constant throughout each example: the length of an eighth note, or a sixteenth note, or a quarter note will not change when the meter changes. The length of the beat, however, will be changing; so be prepared to be very flexible with how you hear the beat.

17.3a

17.3b

17.3. CHANGING COMPOSITE METERS

17.3c Interpret

17.3d Interpret

17.3e

Agitato (♩ = 69)

17.3. CHANGING COMPOSITE METERS

17.3f

Frenetically (♩ = 108)

17.3g

Ridicolosamente (♩ = 76)

17.3. CHANGING COMPOSITE METERS

17.3h

Volante (♩. = 88)

17.3. CHANGING COMPOSITE METERS

17.3i

Expressively (♪. = 138)

17.3j

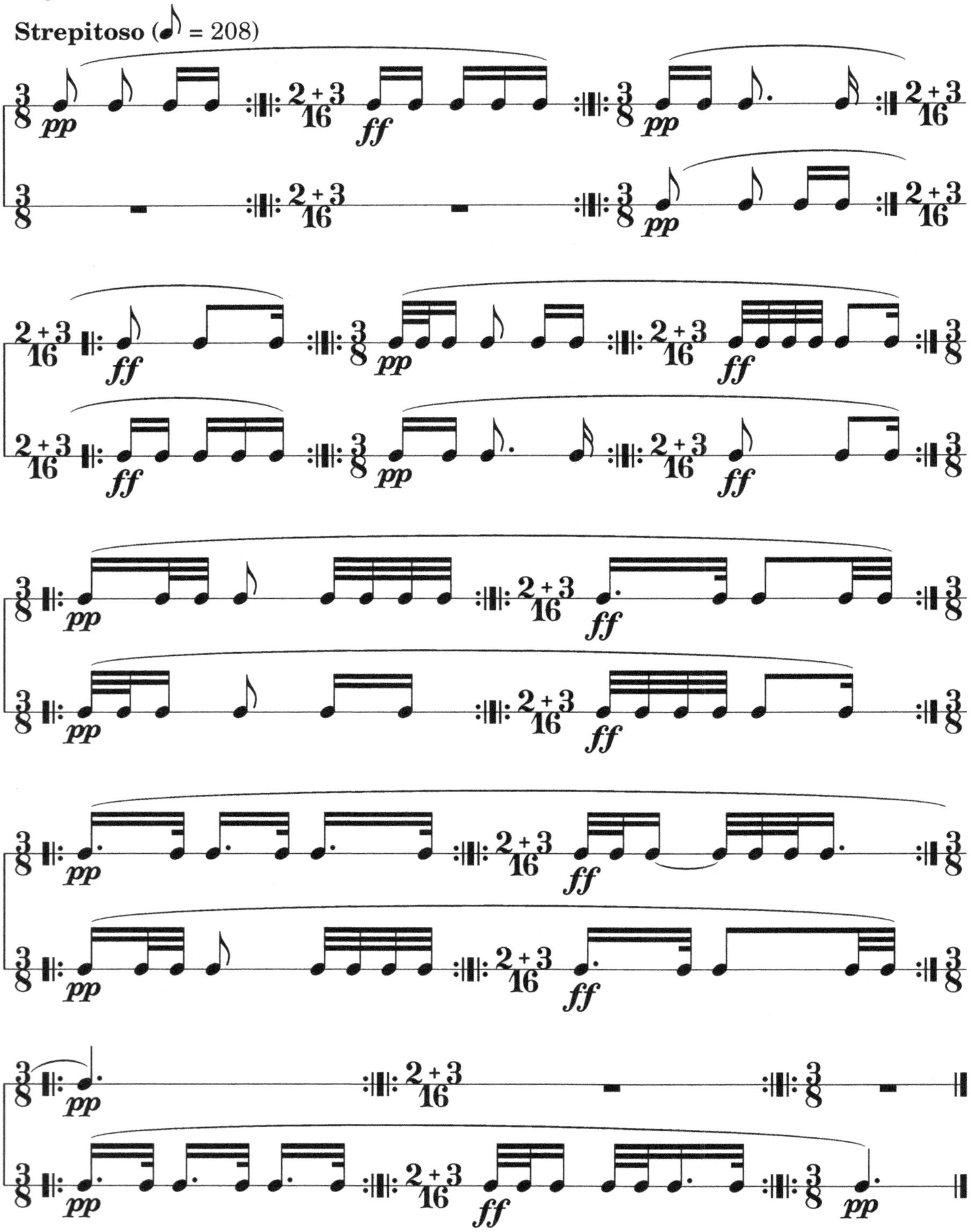
Strepitoso (♪ = 208)
pp
ff
pp
pp
ff
ff
pp
pp
ff
ff
pp
ff
pp
ff
pp
ff
pp
ff
pp
pp
ff
pp

Chapter 18

Modes of the Major Scale

In the first third of the melodic portion of this course (Chapters 2, 4, 6, and 8), we thoroughly explored the sound of diatonic major and minor keys. In the second third (Chapters 10, 12, 14, and 16), we worked with melodic chromaticism, defining chromatic notes as notes not within a particular key signature. In the final third (Chapters 18, 20, 22, and 24), we will move beyond the context of major and minor keys as a primary principle of melodic organization. We will take the first steps of this journey in this chapter, working with diatonic scales other than major and minor. To discover these other scales, we will draw on the concept of mode.

CHAPTER 18. MODES OF THE MAJOR SCALE

A mode is a re-orientation of the notes of a scale around a different center pitch, creating a new scale that is closely related to the initial scale. For example, if you were to play all of the notes of the C major scale, beginning on D and hearing D as the tonic, you would be playing a new scale that is a mode of C major. This new scale has a special name; it is called Dorian. In fact, all of the modes of the major scale have special names.

Ionian Ionian is the first mode of the major scale. Think of Ionian as another name for the major scale.

Dorian Dorian is the second mode of the major scale. Treat the second degree of any major scale as the tonic and you are in Dorian. Dorian is a minor scale with a raised sixth degree. Dorian is the only mode with a symmetrical arrangement of whole steps and half steps.

Phrygian Phrygian is the third mode of the major scale. Treat the third degree of any major scale as the tonic and you are in Phrygian. Phrygian sounds like minor with a lowered second degree.

Lydian Lydian is the fourth mode of the major scale. Treat the fourth degree of any major scale as the tonic and you are in Lydian. Lydian sounds like major with a raised fourth degree.

Mixolydian Mixolydian is the fifth mode of the major scale. Treat the fifth degree of any major scale as the tonic and you are in Mixolydian. Mixolydian sounds like major with a lowered seventh degree. Many popular songs use chords and melodies from Mixolydian.

Aeolian Aeolian is the sixth mode of the major scale. Treat the sixth degree of any major scale as the tonic and you are in Aeolian. Aeolian is the natural minor scale.

Locrian Locrian is the seventh mode of the major scale. Treat the seventh degree of any major scale as the tonic and you are in Locrian. Locrian sounds like minor with lowered second and fifth degrees. Locrian is the least commonly used of all the modes; the lowered fifth degree makes it very unstable.

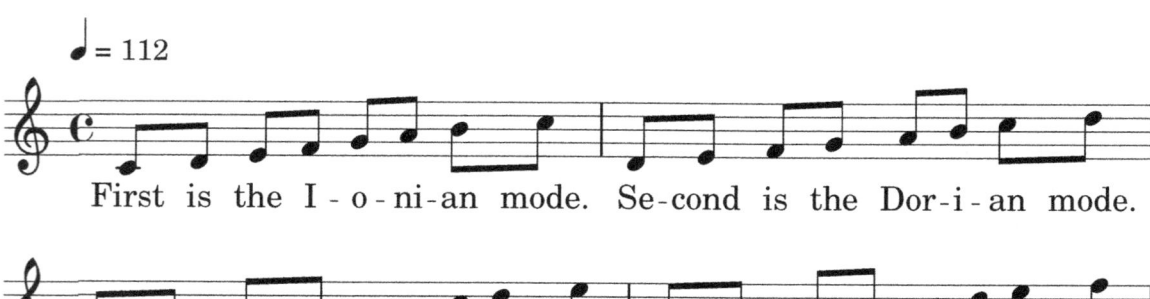

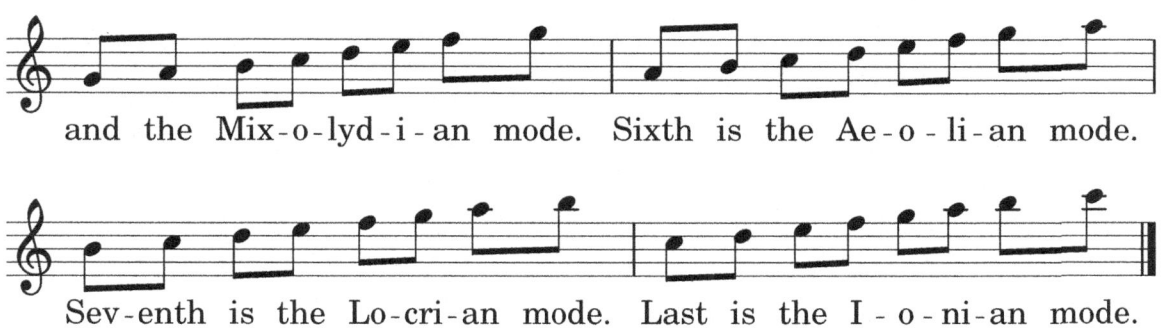

and the Mix-o-lyd-i-an mode. Sixth is the Ae-o-li-an mode.
Sev-enth is the Lo-cri-an mode. Last is the I-o-ni-an mode.

An easy way to memorize the names and order of the different modes is to learn this silly song about pickles by my friend Phala Tracy.[1] Study the lyrics for clever reminders of which modes begin on which scale degrees.

Pickle Song

Phala Tracy

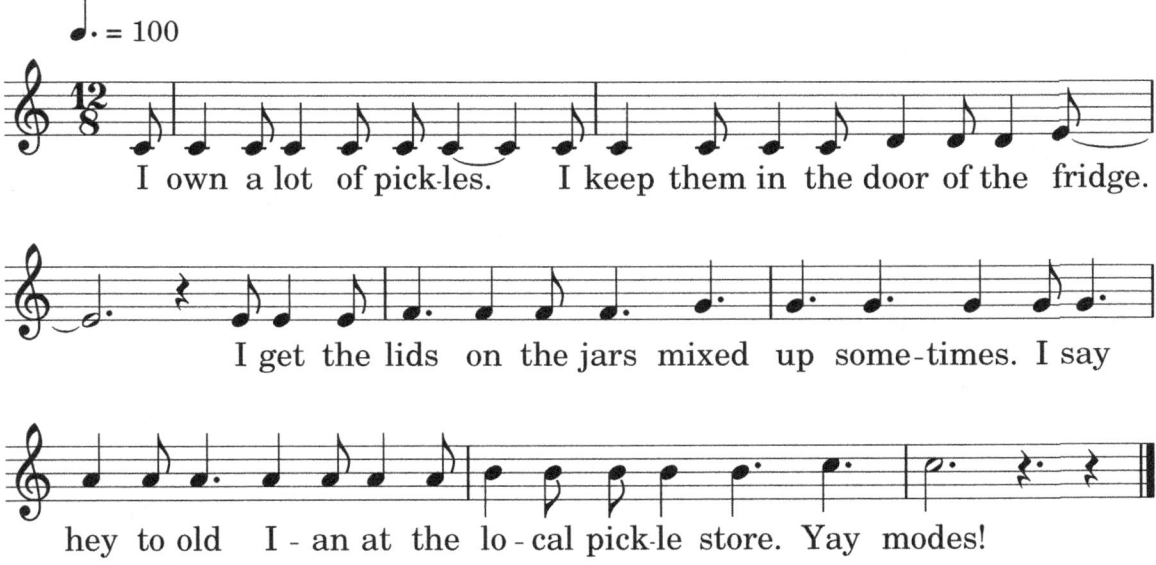

I own a lot of pick-les. I keep them in the door of the fridge.
I get the lids on the jars mixed up some-times. I say
hey to old I - an at the lo-cal pick-le store. Yay modes!

---

[1] This is from an upcoming collection of music theory songs: http://studiofidicina.com. (Used with permission.)

As Ionian and Aeolian are already extensively familiar, being the major and natural minor scales, we will focus on Lydian, Dorian, Mixolydian, and Phrygian here, returning to Locrian in Chapter 20. In Sections 1 and 2, we will introduce each mode as it occurs naturally within a key signature, without the need for accidentals. In Sections 3 and 4, we will work with modes as written in the key signatures of the parallel major and minor, using accidentals to indicate the altered notes of each scale.

18.1 Lydian and Dorian

Lydian Examples

Lydian sounds similar to major, except for the fourth degree. In major, 4 is a perfect fourth above the tonic; in Lydian, 4 is an augmented fourth above the tonic. To play the Lydian scale beginning on C, you would need an F♯, F♯ being an augmented fourth up from C.

Lydian is the fourth mode of the major scale. If you play the notes of the major scale, beginning and ending on its fourth degree, you will have played the Lydian scale. When orienting to the key signature, find the tonic of the major scale. Then find the tonic of the relative Lydian, a fourth above (and a fifth below).

Examples A and E in this section and the next are excerpts of Gregorian chant. These chant melodies are non-metered. I have translated these medieval melodies into modern notation, using eighth and quarter notes to indicate relative duration and fermatas to mark the ends of phrases. The overall approach to rhythm in these examples can be quite free.

18.1a

Gloria

Anonymous

18.1. LYDIAN AND DORIAN

18.1b

Eroico (♩. = 112)

18.1c

Vivamente (♩ = 104)

18.1d

Bacchanalian revelry (♩ = 88)

D.C. al Coda

Dorian Examples

Dorian is a minor mode, having a minor third above the tonic. Dorian is similar to natural minor, except that Dorian has a major sixth above the tonic where natural minor has a minor sixth.

Dorian is the second mode of the major scale. If you play the major scale beginning and ending on its second degree, you will have played the Dorian scale. When orienting to the key signature, find the tonic of the major scale. Then find the tonic of the relative Dorian scale a whole step above.

18.1e

Pange Lingua Gloriosi

Anonymous

18.1f

18.1. LYDIAN AND DORIAN

18.1g

18.1h

Mixed Examples

18.1i

Dorian Service - Magnificat
Thomas Tallis

18.1j

La Mer - No. 2, Jeux de Vagues
Claude Debussy

18.1. LYDIAN AND DORIAN

18.1k

18.1l

18.1m

3 Hungarian Folksongs from Csík - No. 1, The Peacock

Béla Bartók

Specialty Examples

18.1n Duet

18.1o Jam Session

18.1p Analysis

18.1q Figured Bass

18.1r Lead Sheet

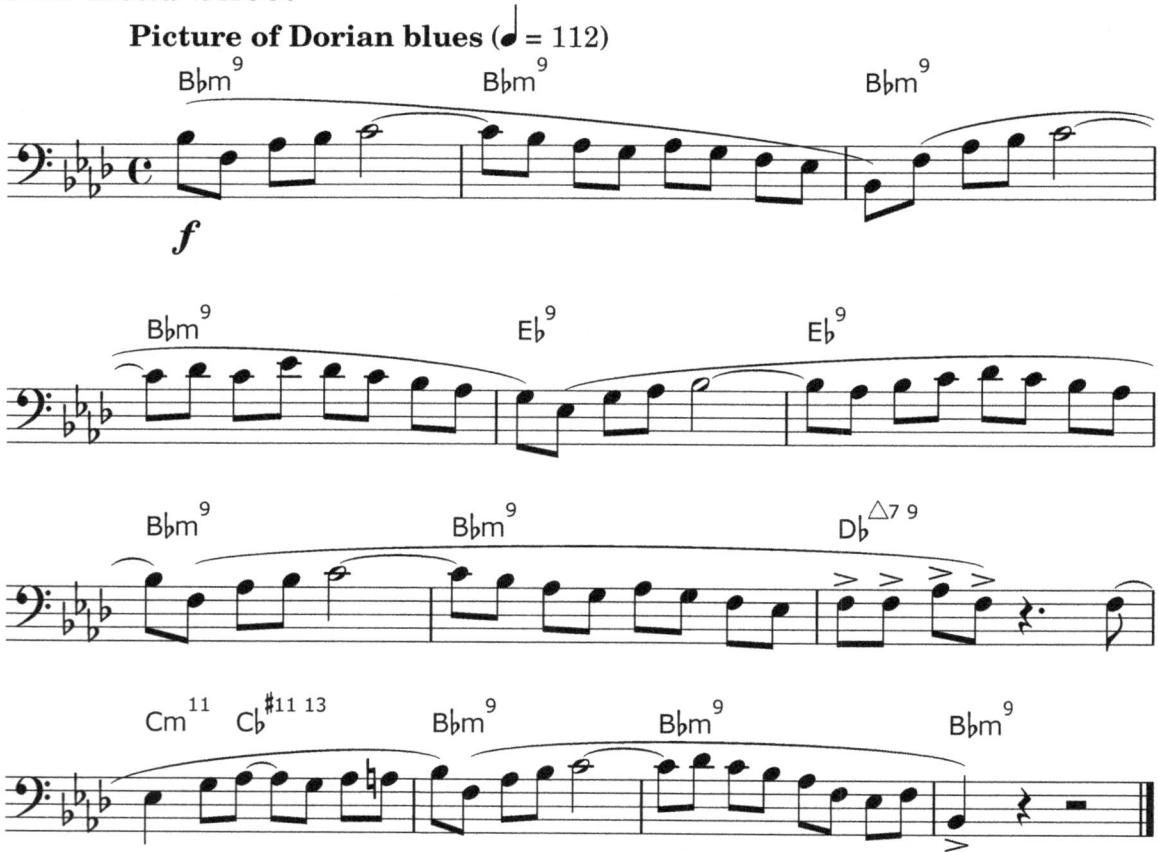

18.1. LYDIAN AND DORIAN

18.1s Find the Music

18.1t Fill in the Blanks

Listening Examples

- Jazz: Miles Davis, "So What," from *Kind of Blue* (1:30–1:57).

- Rock: The Beatles, "Eleanor Rigby," from *Revolver*, written by John Lennon and Paul McCartney.

- Folk Rock: Simon & Garfunkel, "Scarborough Fair/Canticle," from *Parsley, Sage, Rosemary and Thyme*. There are many great arrangements of the traditional song "Scarborough Fair." Here is a classic.

- Pop: Joni Mitchell, "Just Like This Train," from *Court and Spark*. The accompaniment is much more varied, but the vocal melody is purely Lydian.

- Jazz: Regina Carter, "Mandingo Street," from *Rhythms of the Heart* (0:18–0:33), head by Richard Bona. Focus on the violin melody here. By itself, I hear it in Lydian. In the context of the harmonies, I hear it in Dorian.

- Video Games: Rich "Disasterpeace" Vreeland, "Fez - Adventure," performed by The London Philharmonic Orchestra, from *The Greatest Video Game Music 2* (1:01–1:27). Work with three parts here: the bass, the repeating theme, and the slow melody.

18.2 Mixolydian and Phrygian

Mixolydian Examples

Mixolydian is the fifth mode of the major scale. When orienting to the key signature of each example, find the tonic of the major scale. Then find the tonic of the Mixolydian mode a fifth above (or a fourth below). Mixolydian is similar to major, except for the seventh degree, which in mixolydian is lowered. To play Mixolydian on C, you would need a Bb.

18.2a

Verbum caro factum est

Anonymous

18.2. MIXOLYDIAN AND PHRYGIAN

18.2b

18.2c

Old Joe Clark

Traditional

18.2d

Phrygian Examples

Phrygian is another minor mode. It differs from natural minor only in that it has a lowered second degree. This lowered second degree, a half step above the tonic, is the characteristic sound of Phrygian.

18.2e

Salve, festa dies

Anonymous

18.2f

Missa Pangue lingua - No. 1, Kyrie

Josquin des Prez

18.2g

18.2. MIXOLYDIAN AND PHRYGIAN

18.2h

Mixed Examples

18.2i

La Plus Que Lente

Claude Debussy

CHAPTER 18. MODES OF THE MAJOR SCALE

18.2j

18.2. MIXOLYDIAN AND PHRYGIAN

18.2k

18.2l

18.2m

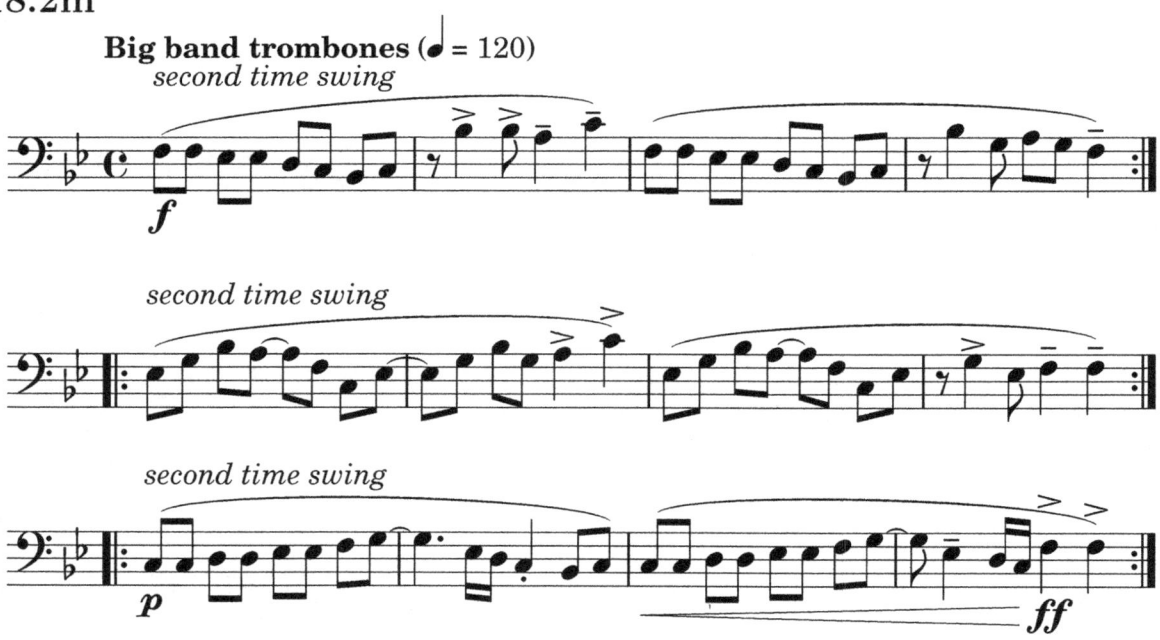

Specialty Examples

18.2n Duet

18.2. MIXOLYDIAN AND PHRYGIAN

18.2o Jam Session

Ecstatically (♩ = 126)

18.2p Analysis

18.2q Figured Bass

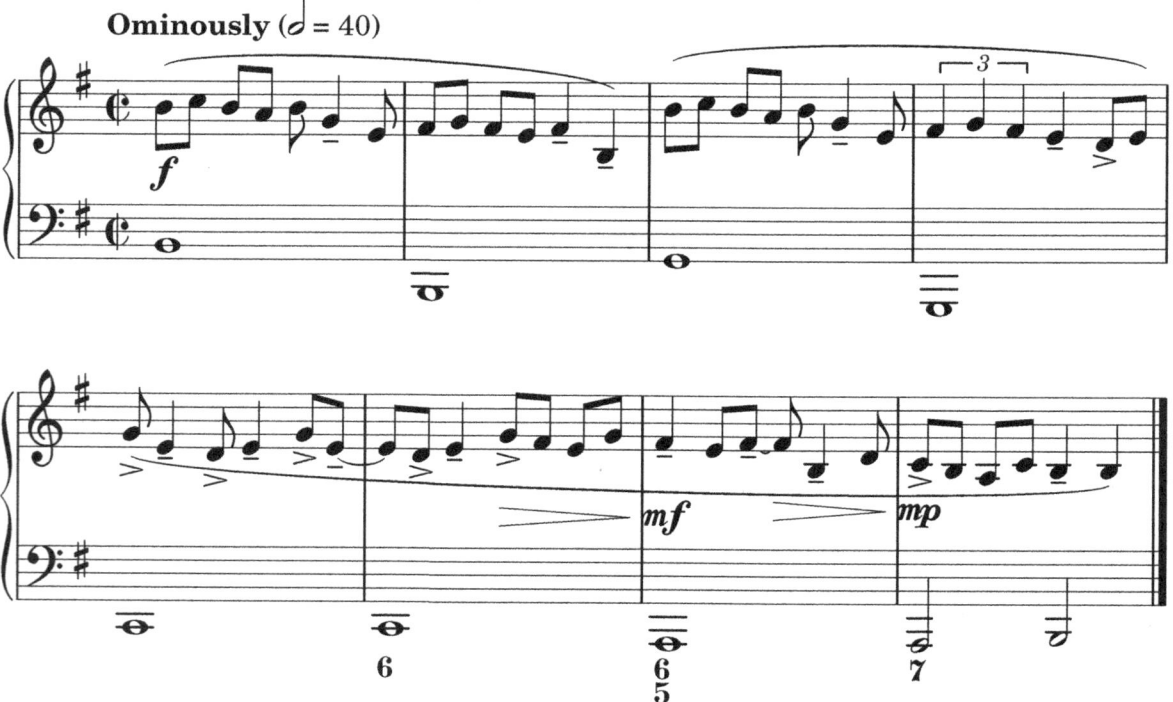

18.2r Lead Sheet

18.2s Find the Music

18.2t Fill in the Blanks

Listening Examples

- Rock: The Beatles, "Norwegian Wood (This Bird Has Flown)," from *Rubber Soul* (0:19–0:39), written by John Lennon and Paul McCartney.

- Psychedelic Soul: Sly and the Family Stone, "Dance to the Music," from *Dance to the Music* (2:16–2:32), written by Sly Stone.

- Progressive Rock: Pink Floyd, "The Trial," from *The Wall* (0:00–0:55), written by Roger Waters and Bob Ezrin.

- Pop: Michael Jackson, "Wanna Be Startin' Somethin'," from *Thriller*.

- Folk: Indigo Girls, "Blood and Fire," from *Indigo Girls*, written by Amy Ray and Emily Saliers.

- Art Rock: Kate Bush, "Love and Anger (Album Version)," from *The Sensual World*.

18.3 Modal Melodies Written in the Parallel Major Key

The examples in this section are written in the parallel major key. Accidentals are used to create the desired mode. For example, if a melody is in D Mixolydian, it is written in D major with natural signs for the seventh scale degree.

I could have written these melodies in key signatures such that fewer or no accidentals were needed. This would likely have made them easier to read. The intent of this section, however, is to stretch your understanding of the relationship between scale and key signature. We are heading toward work with extended modal chromaticism at the end of Chapter 20. This section and the next are necessary stepping stones for that work. I encourage you to practice the melodies in this section and the next in as many ways as you can. Use this as an occasion to stretch your pitch system as much as possible.

Major Modes in the Parallel Major Key

18.3a

William Tell - Overture

Gioachino Rossini

18.3b

18.3c

String Quartet No. 66 in G major, Op. 77

Joseph Haydn

18.3d

18.3. MODAL MELODIES WRITTEN IN THE PARALLEL MAJOR KEY

Minor Modes in the Parallel Major Key

18.3e Eight Improvisations on Hungarian Peasant Songs, Op, 20
Béla Bartók

18.3g Cello Sonata, Op. 5
Ethel Smyth

18.3h

Mixed Examples

18.3i

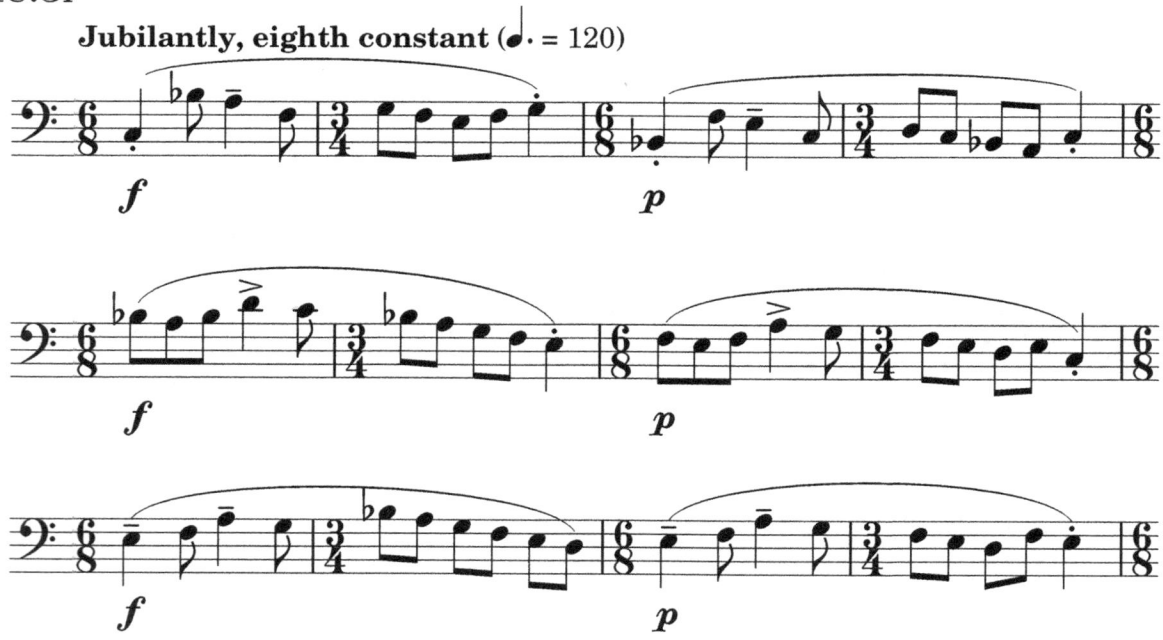

18.3. MODAL MELODIES WRITTEN IN THE PARALLEL MAJOR KEY

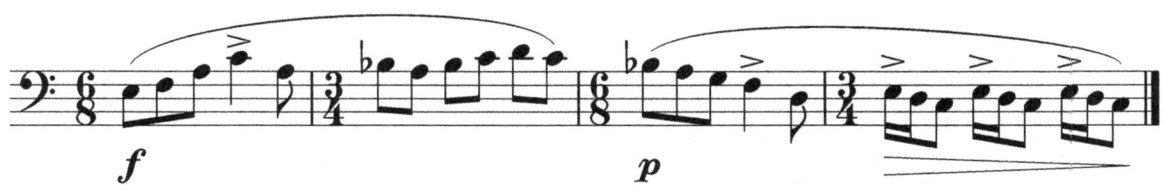

18.3j

18.3k

18.3l

18.3. MODAL MELODIES WRITTEN IN THE PARALLEL MAJOR KEY

18.3m

Specialty Examples

18.3n Trio

Non nobis, Domine

William Byrd

18.3. MODAL MELODIES WRITTEN IN THE PARALLEL MAJOR KEY 227

18.3o Jam Session

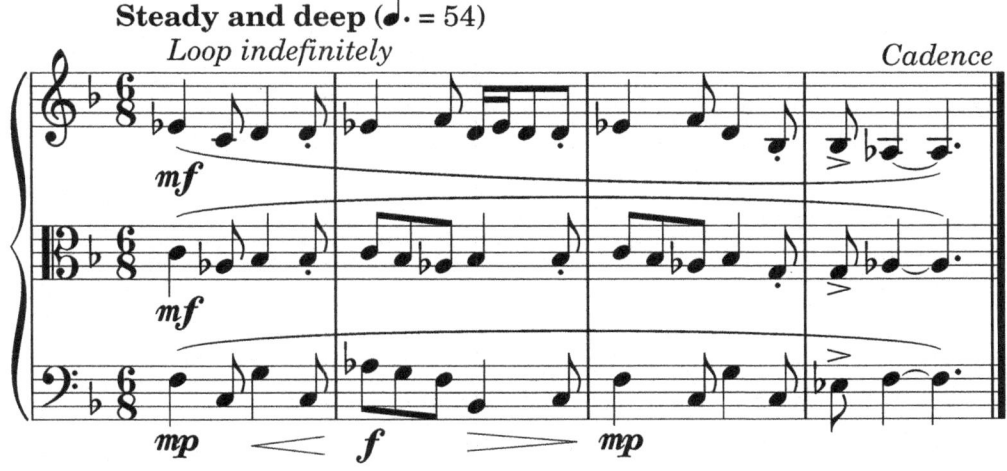

18.3p Analysis

18.3q Figured Bass

18.3r Lead Sheet

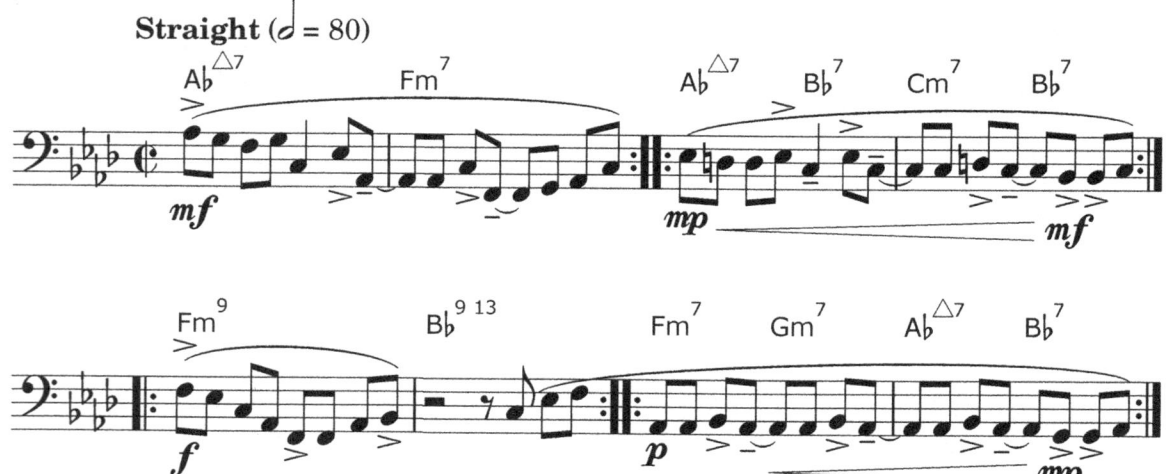

18.3s Find the Music

18.3t Fill in the Blanks

Listening Examples

- Musical Theater: Richard Rodgers and Lorenz Hart, "Johnny One Note," from *Babes in Arms* (original cast recording, 0:05–0:27).

- Folk: Joan Baez, "If I Were a Carpenter," from *Joan Baez Greatest Hits*, written by Tim Hardin.

- Folk Rock: Joni Mitchell, "Chelsea Morning," from *Clouds*.

- Folk Rock: Cheyenne Mize, "Raymaker," from *Among the Grey*.

- Indie Rock: Courtney Barnett, "Are You Looking After Yourself," from *A Sea of Split Peas*.

18.4 Modal Melodies Written in the Parallel Minor Key

The examples in this section are written in the parallel minor key. Use this as an opportunity to stretch your understanding of the relationship between scale and key signature.

Minor Modes in the Parallel Minor Key

18.4a

Sommerlied

Neidhardt von Reuenthal

18.4. MODAL MELODIES WRITTEN IN THE PARALLEL MINOR KEY

18.4b

Second Suite for Military Band - Song without Words

Gustav Holst

18.4c

Sakura

Traditional

18.4d

Waer Dat Men Sich

Traditional

Major Modes in the Parallel Minor

18.4e

18.4. MODAL MELODIES WRITTEN IN THE PARALLEL MINOR KEY 233

Mixed Examples

18.4i

18.4j

Sicilienne, Op. 78

Gabriel Fauré

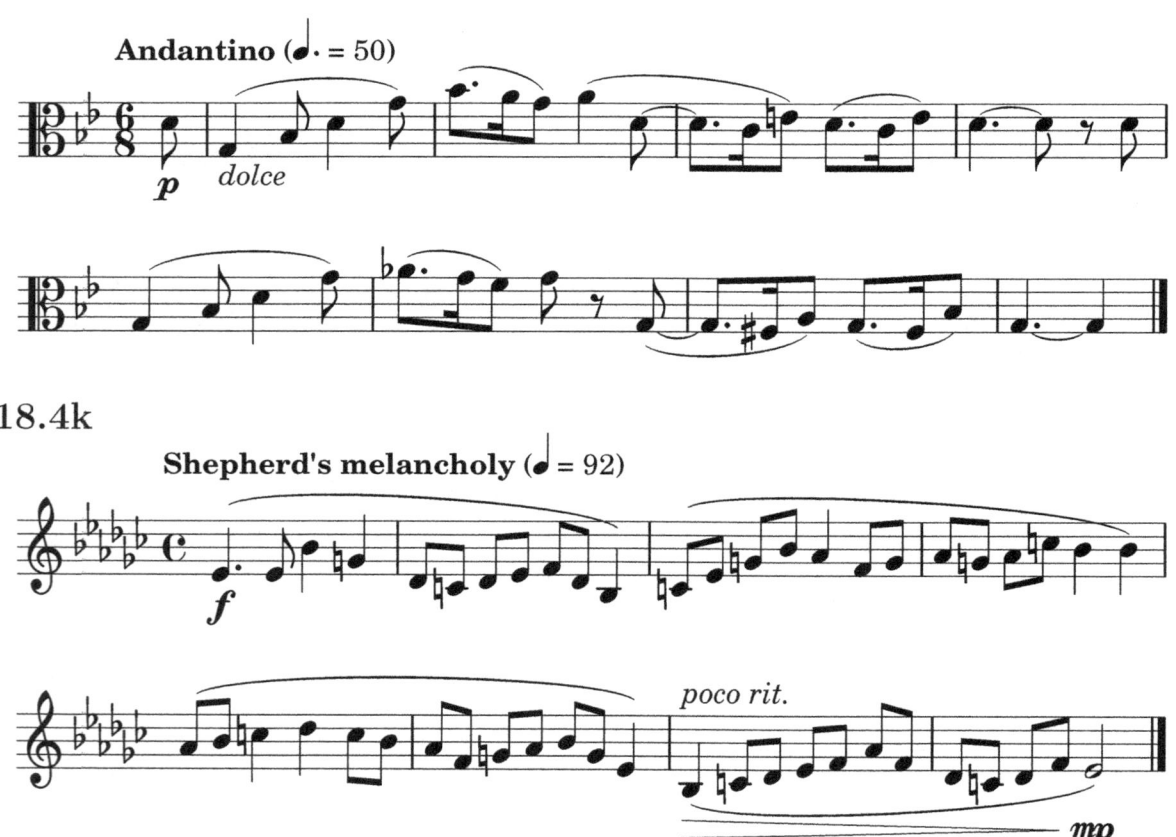

18.4k

18.4. MODAL MELODIES WRITTEN IN THE PARALLEL MINOR KEY

18.4l

18.4m

Specialty Examples

18.4n Duet

18.4. MODAL MELODIES WRITTEN IN THE PARALLEL MINOR KEY

18.4o Jam Session

18.4p Analysis

18.4. MODAL MELODIES WRITTEN IN THE PARALLEL MINOR KEY

18.4q Figured Bass

18.4r Lead Sheet

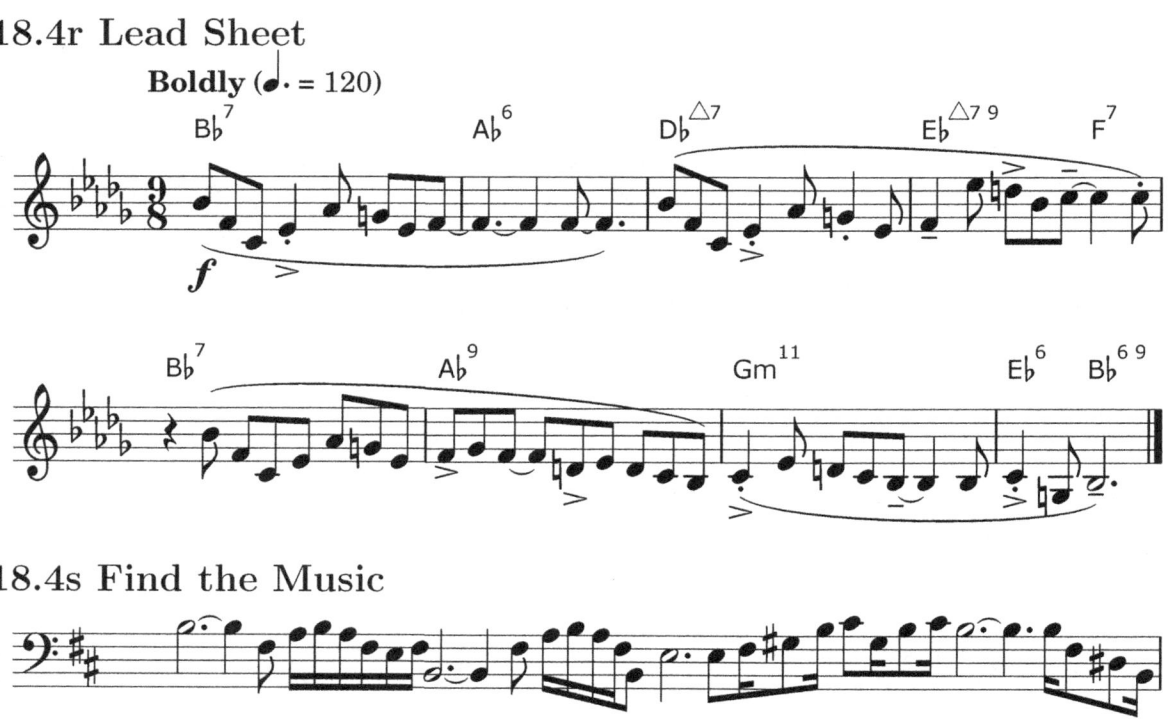

18.4s Find the Music

18.4t Fill in the Blanks

18.4. MODAL MELODIES WRITTEN IN THE PARALLEL MINOR KEY

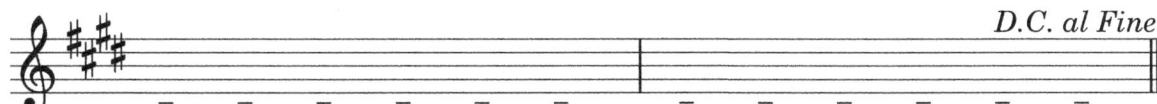

Listening Examples

- Classical: Kassia, "Augustus, the Monarch," in *New Historical Anthology of Music by Women Composers*, Institute of Early Music, Indiana University.

- Rock: The Beatles, "She Came in Through the Bathroom Window," from *Abbey Road* (0:06–0:27), written by John Lennon and Paul McCartney. The melody here is in Dorian while the harmonies reflect Mixolydian.

- Heavy Metal: Queensrÿche, "Scarborough Fair," from *Empire (Bonus Tracks)*. Here is another great arrangement of this traditional song.

- Video Games: Martin O'Donnell and Michael Salvatori, "Halo 3: One Final Effort," performed by The London Philharmonic Orchestra, from *The Greatest Video Game Music* (0:40–0:56). Follow the theme in the violins.

- Video Games: Ari Pulkkinen, "Angry Birds Main Theme," performed by The London Philharmonic Orchestra, from *The Greatest Video Game Music* (0:00–0:34). Focus on the melody in the piano. There is one lowered sixth scale degree near the beginning, evocative of natural minor. After that the melody is in Dorian.

- Folk Rock: Cheyenne Mize, "Among the Grey," from *Among the Grey* (0:00–1:04).

Made in the USA
Columbia, SC
19 August 2020